Wilton shows you how to create

dramatic tier cakes

WILTON ENTERPRISES, INC., WOODRIDGE, ILLINOIS

DECORATOR'S DREAM:

Constructing a beautiful tier cake

To a decorator, there's something magic about a tier cake. To plan, bake and ice the tiers, then assemble them into a structure that's as imposing as a little temple, with tier upon tier rising from the base, is an exhilarating experience—one that's a little intimidating, too, especially if this is your first tier cake.

This book is published to take all the fear out of constructing a tier cake. After you've studied the chapters, one by one, starting at the beginning, you'll have only the fun and excitement of creating an architectural masterpiece. All the secrets of supporting the tiers so they rise steadily and safely from top to bottom are explained.

Much more than that—you'll discover how tiers in correct proportions can create a cake that's a little work of art.

Planning is the key to a beautiful tier cake

A tier cake is nothing but three, four or more single cakes put together—but the putting together does require a careful plan. After you've decided on the design of your cake, take time to bake and ice the tiers carefully. No amount of skillful decorating can disguise an uneven tier or a rough icing job. Pages 4 and 5 tell you all the secrets of preparing even, smoothly iced tiers.

There are only five methods of construction. This book shows you each one in a picture lesson, starting with the easiest and quickest. The purpose of all methods is to support the weight of the tiers. A tier cake can weigh more than 100 pounds! Following the description of each method, you'll see a group of beautiful tier cakes, little to large, constructed as the lesson shows.

Construction is made easy by the many products available to today's decorator. Less than 50 years ago, most tier cake decorators had to laboriously cut their separator plates from wood, fashion the pillars from pastillage or gum paste, trim their tiers to shapes desired, even make their top ornaments by hand. Now modern manufacturing methods have eliminated this time-consuming work. Just glance through the blue pages at the end of this book to see the scores of products that make constructing the tiers almost effortless.

Plan your work as soon as you've decided on the design of your cake. To make planning easy, this book gives a list of the products needed to complete each cake. Make sure they're all on hand, well ahead of decorating day. Estimate the amount of materials needed for baking and decorating the tiers. (Page 4 will help you on this.) Have the variously shaped pans ready for baking the tiers. Then creation of a beautiful tier cake can proceed with ease and enjoyment.

Decorating comes last

This is not an instruction book on decorating although you'll find lots of decorating ideas as you leaf through the pages—and each cake has a note on the way it is trimmed.

A beautifully constructed tier cake is beautiful even when undecorated! Often, only the simplest trim, using basic techniques, is enough to complete the lovely picture.

For many more decorating ideas and descriptions of techniques, see the books listed on the inside front cover.

Frame your beautiful cake with a beautiful base. A silver or crystal tray is ideal, but often not available in the size you need. A foil-covered cake board is the answer. Cut it from three layers of corrugated cardboard at least 4" larger in diameter than the base tier. Tape the three layers together, grain running in opposing directions. Cut Fancifoil 4" larger than the board (you may need to piece). Lay board on foil and pleat edges to conform, then tape. To dress up the board, add doilies or a ruffle (see pages 37 and 40). Ribbon around the edge of the board gives a finished look. Secure it with dots of icing.

For really big cakes, use ½" plywood.

Tier cakes are not just for weddings! They make any occasion more festive and important! Anniversaries, birthdays, graduations, showers, bar mitzvahs—celebrate with a beautiful tier cake.

How to plan a wedding cake.

Consult the bride-to-be. Her desires and preferences come first.

Decide on the design of the cake. Here's the way most decorators help the bride-to-be choose her cake. Go through this book and others that show bridal cakes. The bride-to-be will quickly indicate her choice.

To make the cake truly her own, you may vary the flowers or other trim, use the top ornament she likes best, and decorate in the color scheme she chooses.

Decide on the number of servings needed for the reception. The serving charts on page 66 will be helpful. Almost any cake design can be made larger or smaller.

To increase the number of servings:

Add a base tier. This will give you many more servings.

Increase the size of each tier. For example—change 14", 10" and 6" tiers to 16", 12" and 8".

Add satellite cakes. This gives a lavish effect on the reception table. A bonus—the satellite cakes are very easy to serve.

To decrease the number of servings:

Subtract a tier, usually the base tier.

Reduce the size of the tiers—change from 16", 12" and 8" tiers to 14", 10" and 6" tiers.

Use a styrofoam dummy for the base tier. Decorate it just like a real cake.

Reduce the size of the satellite cakes. Instead of 12" satellites, use 10". Or reduce a 10" satellite to 8".

Write everything down. Decorators who do many wedding cakes have a form for this purpose. It allows space for name of cake design, type and color of flower trim, sizes of tiers and accessories needed, flavors of the cake and filling.

All-important first step

BAKING THE TIERS
START OF A BEAUTIFUL CAKE

After you've decided on the design of your tier cake, it's time to bake the tiers. This may be done a week ahead of time, since tiers may be safely frozen for at least a week, and remain fresh and flavorful. If you're planning a wedding cake, consult the bride-to-be for her choice of flavor. Any mix or recipe is suitable.*

The filling between layers should be the bride's choice, too. Just avoid custard, or any filling that spoils quickly. Fruit fillings may seep into the cake and discolor it. Many decorators choose buttercream.

1. Prepare pans and bake. Thoroughly grease the pans with butter or margarine, or by spraying with non-stick pan release. Now trace the outline of the pans on wax paper, using the point of a scissors, and cut out slightly within the outlines. Fit the wax paper into pans, pressing to smooth. Line the side of the pan with long strips of wax paper cut to the height of the pan. Press in place. This will guarantee that your baked layers will release easily from the pan with no breaks or cracks. Pour batter into the pans, filling one-half to two-thirds full, according to recipe. To help insure a level tier, swirl the batter with the tip of a mixing spoon from center to outer edges. If you wish, wrap the outer sides of the pan with strips of old terry towels wrung out of cold water. Pin in place. This will help to keep the layers level as they bake. Hold filled pan a few inches above counter and drop sharply several times. This will eliminate air bubbles, and assure a fine-grained cake. When layers are baked, set

pans on wire racks to cool from five to ten minutes.

2. Level the layers. For any decorated cake, layers must be completely level with a flat top. If, in spite of your precautions, the layers have risen into a mounded dome or "hump", there are two easy ways to level them. For both methods, *leave the layer in the baking pan.*

Thread method: With a length of fine thread, and starting at one end of layer, move the thread across the layer, pressing it against top of pan and using a back-and-fourth movement. Hump will be cut off. Remove with spatula.

Leveler method. Use the Serrated leveler, page 73. Press the blade against the top of pan and move it across the layer with a sawing motion.

3. Remove layer from pan. Run a spatula around the edges of the pan to loosen sides. Turn layer onto towel-covered cooling rack. The wax paper liner will allow the layer to fall out easily. Peel off liner. Surface will be smooth and unbroken.

Wrap the still-warm layer in plastic wrap, or place in sealed plastic bag. Chill in freezer about 30 minutes, or freeze for up to a week. Chilled or frozen layers are much easier to handle. *If layers are frozen,* allow to stand at room temperature, still wrapped, an hour before filling and icing.

Approximate amounts of batter needed to fill various sizes of pans are given here. We emphasize that *these quantities are only guidelines.* Your own experience is the best guide, since cake recipes and mixes vary widely. One cake mix yields four to six cups of batter. Hexagon, petal and heart tiers require slightly less batter than round tiers.

SHAPE	SIZE	NO. OF CUPS OF BATTER	BAKING TIME	BAKING TEMP.
ROUND	6" x 2"	2	25-30 min.	350°
	8" x 2"	3	30-35	350°
	10" x 2"	6	35-40	350°
	12" x 2"	7½	35-40	350°
	14" x 2"	10	50-55	325°
	16" x 2"	15	55-60	325°
SQUARE	6" x 2"	2	25-30	350°
	8" x 2"	4	35.40	350°
	10" x 2"	6	35-40	350°
	12" x 2"	10	40-45	350°
	14" x 2"	13½	45-50	350°
	16" x 2"	15½	45-50	350°

Approximate amounts of icing needed to cover and decorate tiers. Again we emphasize that *these amounts are only guidelines.* Amounts you need will vary according to icing recipe and type of decoration. *All tiers are two-layers, 3" or 4" high.*

SHAPE	SIZE	CUPS OF ICING	SHAPE	SIZE	CUPS OF ICING
ROUND	6"	3	SQUARE	6"	3½
	8"	4		8"	4½
	10"	5		10"	6
	12"	6		12"	7½
	14"	7¼		14"	9½
	16"	8¾		16"	11

*If you plan to cover the tiers with rolled fondant or candy, use a firm pound cake recipe.

FILLING AND ICING A TIER
to smooth perfection

To cover most cakes, decorators choose buttercream, page 64. It's easy to work with, tastes good, remains soft and toothsome and may be tinted or flavored as you choose. Follow these steps for a perfectly smooth surface. Just a few minutes work will ice a cake as smoothly as those shown in this book.

1. Attach a cardboard cake circle, same size and shape of tier, under every tier before filling and icing. This makes the tier easy to move and prevents knife scratches on tray or separator plate when the tier is cut. Put a few strokes of royal icing on your cake circle, then set chilled bottom layer on it. Press lightly to attach.

2. Pipe a ring of buttercream with tube 12 around top edge of bottom layer. This will act as a "dam" to hold filling in, and keep it from seeping out to discolor icing. Spread filling within ring. Place top layer on bottom layer. Press gently.

3. Set assembled tier on turntable, attaching with strokes of icing. (A turntable makes icing and decorating any cake so much easier, it's almost essential.) Brush any loose crumbs from tier, then brush on hot apricot glaze to seal the surface. Heat apricot jam to boiling, then strain. This will add a pleasant tangy flavor. If you prefer, thin buttercream with milk and cover the tier with a thin layer of icing. Let glaze or icing set about ten minutes until a crust forms.

4. Cover side of tier with icing, using long strokes with a large spatula. Use plenty of icing. Do not attempt to smooth—just cover the side. Turn the turntable as you work.

5. Mound icing in center of top of tier. Spread to cover evenly. Do not smooth.

6. Smooth top of tier. Hold a long metal ruler (or piece of stiff cardboard) upright on edge of tier. Pull ruler toward you, straight across tier. Remove excess icing with spatula.

7. Smooth side of tier. Hold large spatula upright, tip at base of tier. Slowly spin turntable. Remove excess icing with spatula. Trim off any build-up of icing that forms at top of tier with a small spatula.

8. For a super-smooth finish, use the hot knife treatment. Hold large spatula in hot water a minute, wipe off. Put blade flat against top of tier and slowly spin turntable. For side of tier, heat spatula, wipe, and hold flat side of blade against side of tier. Spin turntable to smooth entire side.

Easiest method of all
CENTER COLUMN
CONSTRUCTION
using the
TALL TIER STAND

In this method, the cake rises, tier by tier, with no pillar and dowel support. Just the center columns, almost invisible in the center of the tiers, support the weight. This is the easiest and quickest way to construct a tier cake. It's a very versatile method, too—a petite two-tier, a towering masterpiece or a cake rising above four satellites can be created with the Tall Tier Stand.

Are you planning your first tier cake? Do you need to create a dramatic cake in a hurry? Center Column Construction is for you!

1. We're using the cake on the opposite page as an example, but the procedure will be the same, regardless of the number of the tiers. Our tiers are petal-shaped, 9", 12" and 15", so first prepare cardboard cake circles for each tier. Trace 9", 12" and 15" petal pans on parchment paper. Retrace on larger cardboard cake circles and cut out with a sharp artist's knife. To find the exact center of each tier, fold your paper pattern in quarters. Snip the point to make a center hole. Test the hole for size by slipping it over a column. Enlarge if necessary. Trace hole pattern on prepared cardboard cake circle and cut out. Save your pattern.

2. The base tier of the cake will rest on a 16" plate. To add legs to this plate, turn it upside down. Glue on six legs with "Crazy glue" or other model glue. The legs slip over the six ribs on the plate.

3. Place all tiers on prepared cake circles, attaching with strokes of icing. Ice the tiers. Now make center holes in two lower tiers to receive the columns. Mark the tiers with your cut out patterns. To cut out the hole, press the Cake Corer through the tier right down to the bottom. Hold the corer upright. Remove cake corer and push the upper part down to eject the cake center.

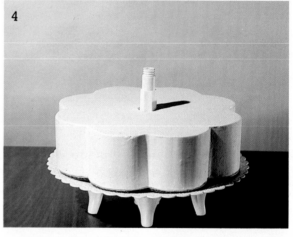

4. Screw a 7¾" column to prepared base plate, attaching with the bottom column bolt from underneath the plate. Slip bottom tier over the column to rest on plate. Set a 14" plate on top of column.

5. Add a second 7¾" column and place 12" tier on plate, slipping over column. Finally, add a 10" plate, securing with top column nut. Place top tier on plate. Mark the backs of all tiers with a dot of icing. For this cake, no further measuring or marking is needed. The next page tells how to decorate.

ROSE PASTEL

Distinguished by its center column construction, each tier of this sweet cake is graced by romantic roses. Rose Pastel is very quick and easy to decorate—the petal shape of the tiers guides the piping. Two lower tiers of Rose Pastel serve 106 guests at a wedding reception.

Accessories you'll need

16", 14" and 10" plates, two 7¾" columns and six glue-on legs, all from the
Tall Tier Stand group, page 74
Top ornament. (Ornaments are shown on pages 75 through 80)

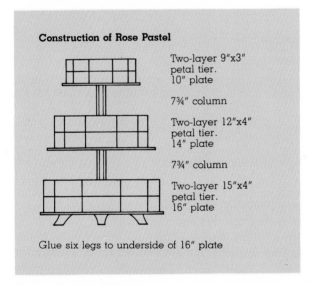

Construction of Rose Pastel

Two-layer 9"x3" petal tier. 10" plate

7¾" column

Two-layer 12"x4" petal tier. 14" plate

7¾" column

Two-layer 15"x4" petal tier. 16" plate

Glue six legs to underside of 16" plate

Decorate Rose Pastel

It's easiest to dis-assemble the tiers and decorate each individually when using the Center Column Construction. Since the plates are slightly concave, rest each on a smaller cake pan. Set top tier on a 6" or 8" pan, middle tier on a 10" pan.

To prevent the tiers from shifting, lay a damp folded towel or piece of thin foam over the pans. Bottom tier is decorated on its plate.

Pipe the roses ahead in royal icing. The rest of the decorating goes quickly. Bottom shell borders, garlands and curved shells finish the tiers. To conceal the legs, we curved an artificial garland of greens below the base tier. Set top ornament in place and admire your handiwork!

Easiest method of all
CENTER COLUMN CONSTRUCTION
DAISY

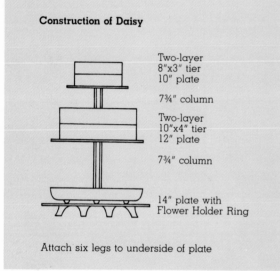

Construction of Daisy

Two-layer
8"x3" tier
10" plate

7¾" column

Two-layer
10"x4" tier
12" plate

7¾" column

14" plate with
Flower Holder Ring

Attach six legs to underside of plate

Daisy is one of the sweetest, prettiest cakes you could decorate for a small intimate wedding reception, a bridal shower or, with a change of ornament, an important party. It's dessert and centerpiece in one, with the tiers rising above a circle of fluffy gum paste daisies. The Gum Paste Flower kit, page 67, shows the easy way of making these. Of course you may substitute fresh or fabric flowers.

Two tiers of Daisy serve 78 guests at a wedding reception, or 24 at a party.

Using the Flower Holder Ring

Arrange your flowers in the Flower Holder Ring. Just wedge blocks of styrofoam in the ring and stick the stems of the flowers into it. If you choose fresh flowers, use florists' clay instead of styrofoam, moisten with water, then arrange the flowers. The ring slips easily over the center column that separates the plates of the Tall Tier Stand.

Accessories you'll need

Two 7¾" columns, 14", 12" and 10" plates, six glue-on legs—all from the Tall Tier Stand group, page 74

Top ornament (ornaments are shown on pages 75 through 80)

Gum Paste Flower kit and accessories for making daisies, page 67

Flower Holder Ring, page 69

Decorate Daisy

Flowers are the featured trim, so the rest of the decorating is simple and done with speedy star tubes. Divide each tier into sixths, pipe shell borders, then add garlands and strings. To assemble, glue legs to the bottom of the 14" plate, just as shown on page 6. Secure a 7¾" column to this plate, put the flower arrangement on the plate, then add the 12" plate. Set 10" tier on plate, attach second column and 10" plate. Finally set 8" tier in position.

For information on purchasing products, please see inside front cover

10

SUNNY MORNING

Construction of Sunny Morning

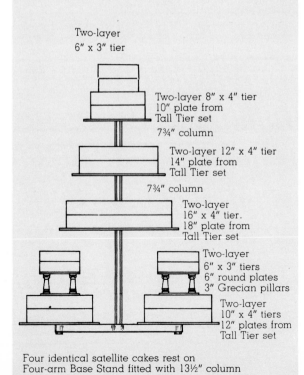

Two-layer
6" x 3" tier

Two-layer 8" x 4" tier
10" plate from
Tall Tier set

7¾" column

Two-layer 12" x 4" tier
14" plate from
Tall Tier set

7¾" column

Two-layer
16" x 4" tier.
18" plate from
Tall Tier set

Two-layer
6" x 3" tiers
6" round plates
3" Grecian pillars

Two-layer
10" x 4" tiers
12" plates from
Tall Tier set

Four identical satellite cakes rest on
Four-arm Base Stand fitted with 13½" column

A mid-summer dream of a bridal cake! The lofty main cake seems to float above four surrounding small tier cakes. The Tall Tier Stand and Four-arm base make this magic possible. Garden touches include the miniature fence, the picket arch that frames the couple and four dainty cherubs. Three lower tiers of main cake serve 216 guests. Each satellite cake serves 64 for a total of 472 servings. A new bride suggests these cakes be given to the parents and grandparents of the couple.

Please note: satellite cakes are constructed in the dowel-and-pillar method, page 21.

Building with the Four-arm base stand

This addition to the Tall Tier Stand is easy to use— and is a quick way to make a modestly sized cake much larger. Add either a 7¾" or a 13½" column to the center opening of the stand by securing it with the base nut that comes with the stand. Now set a 16" plate on the attached pillar and proceed with construction exactly as shown on page 6. (On Sunny Morning we used an 18" plate as the base plate for the main cake, so the six legs attached to the plate were snapped off.)

On each of the four arms of the stand, set plates for satellite cakes. You may use 8", 10" or 12" plates. Weight of the cakes will hold the plates securely.

Accessories you'll need

For main cake:

18", 14" and 10" plates plus two 7¾" columns, all from the Tall Tier Stand group, page 74

Picket Arch, page 68

Formal Figures, page 68

Eight Angelinos, page 68

Old-Fashioned Garden fence, page 68

For four satellite cakes:

Four 12" plates, Four-arm Base Stand and 13½" column, all from the Tall Tier Stand group, page 74

Four Angel Fountains, page 68

Sixteen 3" Grecian Pillars, page 71

Eight 6" Round Separator Plates, page 70

Decorate Sunny Morning

Almost all trim is done with speedy star tubes and quick drop flowers. On satellite cakes, do shell borders, then pipe zigzag garlands on both tiers and trim with drop flowers and string work. It's best to pipe garlands on 6" tiers at the reception room, since they hang below bottom of tiers.

The main cake has harmonizing trim. 16" and 12" tiers are bordered with shells, then garlands, string and flower trim are added. Base border of 8" tier is a series of puff garlands. Stringwork trims both 8" and 6" tiers. The arch, fence and Angelinos all have flower trim.

Daisy Field shows how center column construction at its simplest can produce a cake of great charm. Just follow the directions on page 6. You saw it in a previous book—it's still one of our most popular designs. Serve Daisy Field to 140 guests.

Decorate Daisy Field. Final decoration is very quick—just make lots of royal icing daisies ahead of time. Each tier is trimmed in the same way. Pipe puffy tube 32 shell borders at base, then frame each shell with tube 76 curves. Add curves of tiny dots above the shells. Do simple shell borders at top of tiers. The center column allows uninterrupted spaces for your "fields" of daisies. Attach them on little mounds of icing.

Accessories you'll need

16", 12" and 8" plates, two 7¾" columns and six glue-on legs, all from the Tall tier stand group, page 74

Top ornament (pages 75-80)

Prelude, one of your all-time favorites is another example of the versatility of the Tall tier stand. Construct it just as shown on pages 6 and 11. This romantic cake serves 252 guests.

Decorate Prelude simply and effectively with ruffled garlands, shell borders and a profusion of snow-white roses. The crowning touch is a rose-covered heart. To make it cut the heart from rolled gum paste with a 4" cutter. Cut out the center with a 2½" cutter. Attach a Y-shaped wire to the back to stick into tier, then add a second identical heart for strength. Secure made-ahead royal icing roses.

Accessories you'll need

For main cake, 16", 12" and 8" plates and two 7¾" columns from the Tall tier set, page 74

For satellite cakes, Four-arm base stand fitted with a 6½" column and four 10" plates from the Tall tier stand group, page 74.

Four cupid figures, page 68

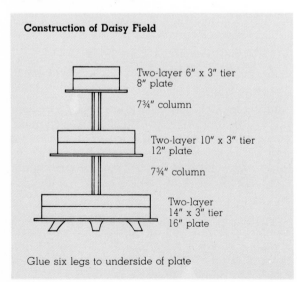

Construction of Daisy Field

Two-layer 6" x 3" tier
8" plate

7¾" column

Two-layer 10" x 3" tier
12" plate

7¾" column

Two-layer
14" x 3" tier
16" plate

Glue six legs to underside of plate

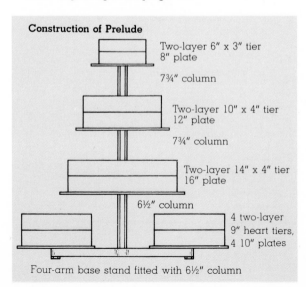

Construction of Prelude

Two-layer 6" x 3" tier
8" plate

7¾" column

Two-layer 10" x 4" tier
12" plate

7¾" column

Two-layer 14" x 4" tier
16" plate

6½" column

4 two-layer
9" heart tiers,
4 10" plates

Four-arm base stand fitted with 6½" column

Easiest method of all
CENTER COLUMN CONSTRUCTION

ROSEBUD

Tiers of this sweet shower cake are baked in 8″ and 10½″ ring pans, covered with rolled fondant and assembled with components of the Tall tier stand. Quickest construction of all—the openings in the ring tiers are ready-made to receive the center column. Fast star tubes do all the trim, made-ahead roses crown the tiers. Refer to page 6 for basic construction. Rosebud serves 50 party guests.

Construction and accessories needed

Attach Musical trio to plate of 3¼″ Heart base, page 68

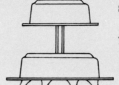

8″ ring tier, page 72
10″ plate, page 74

7¾″ column, page 74

10½″ ring tier, page 72
14″ plate, page 74

Attach six glue-on legs, page 74, to underside of plate

2. Repeat this process for each tier, working from largest to smallest tier. Top tier is left untouched. Always mark the leg position by pressing with the separator plate for the tier above.

Quick and very easy
PUSH-IN LEG
CONSTRUCTION
using the
CRYSTAL CLEAR DIVIDER SET

Here is a second very easy way to construct a tier cake. Legs attach to separator plates and push right through the tiers down to the plate below. These legs support all the weight of the tiers above. The result is a strong, stable support for even the tallest tier cake. A beautiful by-product—the legs are clear plastic, so the tiers seem to float, one above the other. See the exquisite cakes on the pages that follow—then go on to create your own masterpieces. Two lengths of legs make construction very versatile.

Here we are using 14″, 10″ and 6″ round tiers.

3. Place each iced upper tier on its separator plate. Attach by stroking plate with royal icing. Mark center back and center front of all tiers with dots of icing—two dots for back, one for front. Make sure that these marks are midway between two leg projections on the plate. Make marks as you view tier at eye level. Swivel the tier, if necessary, while icing on plate is still wet.

1. Start by icing the tiers as shown on page 5. Place bottom tier on foil covered cake board or serving tray. Attach by stroking the cake board with royal icing. Mark the position of the legs. Using the separator plate *for the next tier above*, projections down, gently press it onto the tier, making sure it is centered. Lift plate away. The projections will leave marks on the icing to guide position of legs when you assemble the tiers.

4. Now decorate each tier. The front and back marks will be guides in placing your trim. Assemble the cake on the reception table. Insert legs in leg projections below separator plate. Start with the tier above base tier. Hold it above base tier, making sure that legs are directly above marks on top of base tier. Push straight down until legs touch cake board. Continue adding tiers in the same way until cake is completely assembled.

Quick and very easy
PUSH-IN LEG CONSTRUCTION
TINY TIER CAKES

A birthday cake is much more impressive when it's tiered! Construct this little showpiece exactly as shown on the facing page. Pipe roses and rose buds ahead in royal icing. Then trim each tier with shell borders and dropped strings. Place make-it-yourself heart ornament on top tier. Add the flowers on mounds of icing. Push-in Holders carry the candles that ring the bottom tier. Serve to twelve party guests.

A shower centerpiece draws admiration from the guests. Construct the cake as shown on the opposite page. Then pose it in a circle of fresh flowers arranged in the Flower Holder Ring. (See page 8). A quick and easy cake becomes a sensation! Decorate the tiers with shell borders, ruffles and dropped strings. To serve to twelve, lift the cake, on its plate, from the flowers. Present the flower arrangement to the guest of honor.

Construction and accessories needed

Heart Mini-tier set, page 72
Bake single-layer tiers

4" Filigree Heart and
top plate from
3¼" Heart Base, page 68

Push-in Candle Holders, page 68

Glue Filigree Heart to top plate from ornament base

Construction and accessories needed

Party Parasol, page 68

Round Mini-tier set, page 72
Bake single-layer tiers

Base tier rests on two
8" Round plates, page 70,
fitted with 3" Crystal-look
pillars, page 71

Flower Holder Ring, page 69,
fits over bottom plate

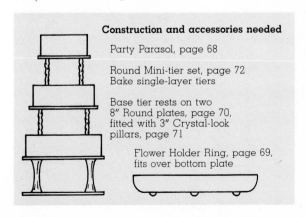

15

16

Quick and very easy
PUSH-IN LEG CONSTRUCTION

NOSEGAY

Nosegay is a stunning bridal cake, lavishly trimmed with lattice and bows. Four dainty nosegays rest on the bottom tier, another is placed within pillars.

For all its elegance and beauty, Nosegay is a very easy cake to construct. Just follow the directions on page 14. The large square base tier gives it a distinctive silhouette, and allows for a generous number of servings. Three lower tiers of Nosegay serve 340 wedding guests.

Accessories you'll need

*Top ornament (ornaments are shown
on pages 75 through 80)
8", 12" and 16" plates, four 7½" legs
and eight 9" legs, all from
the Crystal Clear Divider group, page 74
8" Round Doilies, florist tape
and fine wire, page 67
for making nosegays
Five plates from 4¼" Heart bases, page 68,
(to place nosegays on)*

Decorate Nosegay

Make the nosegays first. Pipe royal icing flowers, dry and mount on wire stems. Pipe leaves on wire stems. Twist stems together and insert in hole cut in center of doily. Bind with florist tape. When cake is decorated, place plates on cake, then set nosegays on plates.

Star tubes make shell borders on all tiers and pipe the scalloped circles on tier tops. Drop double strings to guide all lattice. On lower string, pipe zigzag garlands, then pipe lattice from upper string to garland. To guide the slanted groups of lattice on base tier, make a mark 7½" in from each corner at top edge of tier. Make a second series of marks on each corner, 1½" up from bottom. Lightly mark a line connecting the marks.

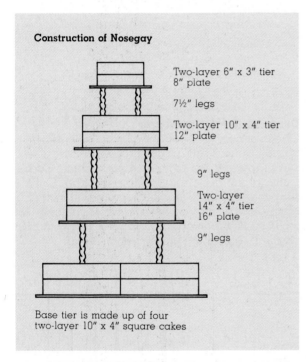

Construction of Nosegay

Two-layer 6" x 3" tier
8" plate

7½" legs

Two-layer 10" x 4" tier
12" plate

9" legs

Two-layer
14" x 4" tier
16" plate

9" legs

Base tier is made up of four
two-layer 10" x 4" square cakes

For information on purchasing products, please see inside front cover

QUEEN OF HEARTS

Queen of Hearts rises like a shimmering tower from a base of four satellite cakes. To accomplish this glorious vision, just use the Crystal Clear Divider Set and the basic method shown on page 14. The diagram below shows how the satellite cakes are made an integral part of the main cake. Queen of Hearts serves 400, not counting the top tier, to be frozen for the first anniversary.

Accessories you'll need
For main cake:

Top ornament (ornaments are shown on pages 75 through 80)

10", 12", 14" and 16" plates, eight 7½" legs and eight 9" legs, all from the Crystal Clear Divider group, page 74

Heart Cookie cutters, page 73 (to use as pattern presses)

For satellite cakes:

Four Musical Trio figures, page 68

Four Filigree Hearts, page 68

Four 12" plates from Crystal Clear Divider group, page 74

16 Crystal-look Feet, page 70 (to fit over pillar projections on plates)

Decorate Queen of Hearts
Queen of Hearts appears elaborate, but the trim is quickly done. Only round tubes are used. Measure and mark the tiers, then press Heart Cookie Cutters into the icing to define the trim. Outline shapes with tube 2, then fill in areas with fast Philippine "sotas", tiny swirls and curves of icing. No top borders are needed. Finish the tiers with bulb borders, garlands, string and beading.

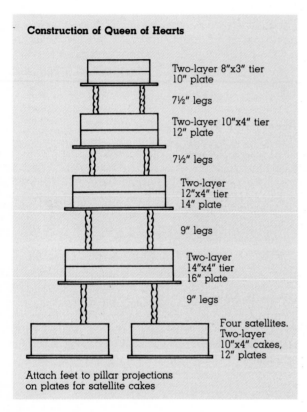

Construction of Queen of Hearts

Two-layer 8"x3" tier
10" plate

7½" legs

Two-layer 10"x4" tier
12" plate

7½" legs

Two-layer 12"x4" tier
14" plate

9" legs

Two-layer 14"x4" tier
16" plate

9" legs

Four satellites. Two-layer 10"x4" cakes, 12" plates

Attach feet to pillar projections on plates for satellite cakes

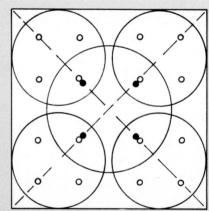

Joining satellite cakes to main cake
Attach feet to leg projections of four 12"plates. Attach satellite cakes to plates. Draw a 25" square on newspaper. Draw an "X" from opposite corners of square. Set satellite cakes within square, edges of plates touching edges of square. Make sure two opposite feet of each are over "X". Now lightly press a 16" plate on the four satellite cakes to mark position of legs. The leg projections on the 16" plate should be over the "X". This will give stability to the cake.

Quick and very easy
PUSH-IN LEG CONSTRUCTION

SUNSHINE

The sweetest, sunniest cake you could decorate for her birthday! Push-in leg construction, page 14, gives it height and importance, shiny poured fondant makes it glow. Add candles and dainty flowers and you have a little beauty for a birthday centerpiece. Serve Sunshine to 28 party guests.

Accessories you'll need

8" plate and four 7½" legs
from the Crystal clear divider set, page 74
Cake dividing set, page 73

Decorate Sunshine

Pipe many royal icing drop flowers. Cover both tiers with buttercream, then Quick poured fondant as described on page 64. Using the Cake dividing set, divide both tiers into eights and mark midway on sides. Make a 3" x 4" oval pattern from folded paper. Transfer to sides of lower tier, following marks. Cut scalloped pattern from an 8" folded paper circle and transfer to top of tier.

Assemble tiers with Crystal clear legs and plate. Pipe shell borders on both tiers, then pipe garlands on lower halves of ovals and on top tier. Complete remaining decorating with tube 1. Add flowers to cover garlands and arrange the birthday candles.

Construction of Sunshine

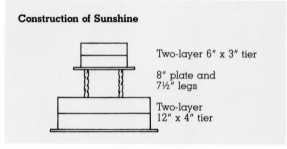

Two-layer 6" x 3" tier

8" plate and 7½" legs

Two-layer 12" x 4" tier

20

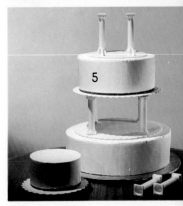

Most dramatic method

DOWEL-PLUS-PILLAR

CONSTRUCTION

using

SEPARATOR PLATES
AND PILLARS

With this popular construction, each tier is separated by pillars so that even a modestly sized cake rises to a dramatic height. It's most important to remember that none of the tiers should bear any weight at all. For this reason, dowel rods are inserted into all lower tiers to support the weight of the tiers above. Dowel-plus-pillar construction is very versatile, too. Just glance at pages 69 and 71 to see the variety of pillars available. It's easy to give your cake a personality of its own.

Follow the steps below carefully and you'll be confident that your cake will stand tall and secure on the reception table. We're using two-layer round tiers, 14", 10" and 6" in diameter, with 12" and 8" separator plates. The method is the same, regardless of the number or sizes of tiers.

1. Put a few strokes of royal icing on your prepared cake board or tray, then set the iced 14" tier on it, making sure it is centered. Center a 10" cake circle (one size smaller than the separator plate above) on tier top and press lightly to imprint the icing. Remove cake circle. Use this circle to guide the insertion of seven ¼" dowel rods*. First push one dowel rod straight down through tier until it touches the cake board below. Make a knife-scratch on the rod to mark exact height of tier *(not including icing)*. Pull dowel rod out. Cut all rods the exact same length, using scratch on first one as a guide. Use a pipe cutter or a pruning shears. Now insert all seven rods into tier, spacing evenly around circle, and pushing straight down until each touches the cake board. The dowel rods will slide into the tier more easily if you first moisten them by wiping with a damp cloth.

2. Attach 10" tier to 12" separator plate by putting a few strokes of royal icing on plate. Since separator plate above is 8", use a 6" cake circle to imprint exact center of tier. Remove cake circle. Measure and cut five dowel rods, just as in Step 1. Insert dowels around marked circle. Remove top 6" tier from its cardboard cake circle by sliding a spatula under tier. Stroke 8" separator plate with royal icing and center tier on plate. Ridges on plate will hold tier securely.

3. This tier, cut in half, shows dowel rods within. Others are not visible.

4. Construct the tiers with pillars and plates. *Make sure all plates are centered* on tiers. Place 12" plate on 14" tier top, projections up. Attach pillars. Set 10" tier, on its plate on pillars.

To keep the separator plate from sticking to the icing when you take cake apart for serving, sprinkle center of tier with coconut, or sift it with confectioners' sugar.

5. Center 8" plate on 10" tier top, projections up. *Most important:* Be sure pillar projections on this plate line up with pillars below. Observe carefully at eye level. Attach pillars, then add top 6" tier, on plate. Now is the time to mark exact center back of each tier with two dots of icing. To make sure all decorations will line up, mark center fronts with one dot of icing. Take tiers apart by lifting off pillars to decorate.

*The general rule for number of dowel rods is: the larger and more numerous the tiers, the more dowels needed. If the tier above is 10" or less, use seven ¼" dowels. Increase the number of dowels by two for each 2" larger tier. For example: If tier above is 12" in diameter, use nine dowels. If tier above is 14" in diameter, use eleven dowels. For really big cakes with many tiers, use ½" dowel rods in base tier. Cut with a coping saw.

21

BELL FLOWER

Bell Flower is a perfect example of the dowel-and-pillar construction. Although it is of medium size, this cake appears very impressive with the tiers supported by 7" pillars. Within each set of pillars is a pretty little tableau—on the base tier, the images of the bride and groom, above them, dainty flowers in a bell-shaped vase. Crowning the top is a joyous little cherub, prophesying happiness for the loving couple. Construct Bell Flower just as shown on page 21. Two lower tiers serve 200 guests at a wedding reception.

Accessories you'll need

Frolicking cherub, page 68

Harvest cherub separator set, page 71

2¾" bell and plate from 3½" heart base for flower vase, page 68

Four 7" Corinthian pillars, page 71

Formal figures
place on plate from 4½" heart base, page 68

Two 13" square plates, page 70

Dowel rods, page 70

Decorate Bell Flower

Make many lily-shaped bell flowers (blue bells) in advance in royal icing, then decorating the cake is easy. Measuring is important for this cake. On base tier make a mark 2½" in from each corner, 1" below top. Divide center spaces into fourths. This will guide garlands. On middle tier, make marks 2" from each corner. Divide base of top tier into eighths. Now do all the piping with fast star tubes, using marks as guides.

Glue bell to small ornament plate to use as a vase for flowers mounted on wire stems. Add flowers to all tiers, attaching on mounds of icing. Bell Flower is beautifully complete—and the centerpiece of the wedding reception.

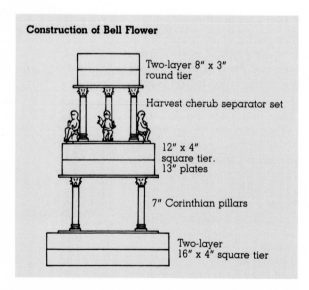

Construction of Bell Flower

Two-layer 8" x 3" round tier

Harvest cherub separator set

12" x 4" square tier. 13" plates

7" Corinthian pillars

Two-layer 16" x 4" square tier

For information on purchasing products, please see inside front cover

23

Most dramatic method
DOWEL-AND-PILLAR CONSTRUCTION
CHOCOLATE JOY

Construction of Chocolate Joy

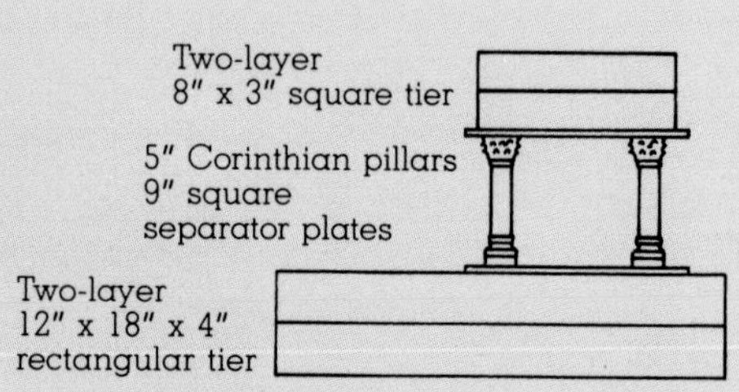

Two-layer
8" x 3" square tier

5" Corinthian pillars
9" square
separator plates

Two-layer
12" x 18" x 4"
rectangular tier

Set lower separator plate 1½" in from
one short side of base tier

Chocolate Joy turns his birthday into a big celebration! Here's everything he ever wanted for his birthday cake—two of his favorite flavors, lots of servings, a show-off ornament—all put together with a big curve of chocolate roses.

The dowel-and-pillar construction gives drama to this tailored cake by lifting the top tier well above the large base tier. Construct Chocolate Joy just as shown on page 21, but note that the upper tier is set to one side to give space for the message. Of course, you can change it into a shower cake, or a petite wedding cake or a centerpiece for any big party by varying the color and ornament. Chocolate Joy serves 66 party guests.

Accessories you'll need

Top ornament, page 78

Push-in candle holders, page 68

Two 9" square separator plates, page 70

Four 5" Corinthian pillars, page 71

Dowel rods, page 70

Decorate Chocolate Joy

First make lots of chocolate buttercream roses using tubes 102, 104 and 124. Air-dry or freeze. To carry out the warm color scheme, paint the pillars, plates and ornament with thinned royal icing and a small artist's brush. You may need to give them a second coat to get a good covering.

The rest of the decorating is quick and easy, all done with star tubes. Pipe shell borders and dropped strings on both tiers. After the lower separator plate is in position, mark a curve on the base tier as a guide for placing the roses. Prop the roses on the sides of the tiers with toothpicks, if necessary. Insert candles, in holders, into top tier, add ornament and trim with roses. Light up the birthday party!

For information on purchasing products, please see inside front cover

Most dramatic method
DOWEL-AND-PILLAR CONSTRUCTION
*Showpieces from
another book*

Morning Song displays the Dowel-and-pillar method at its most imposing and dramatic. The tiers of the main cake are lifted on tall Arched pillars that enclose an ornament. Six surrounding satellite cakes add more drama—and more servings. Adapt this beautiful cake for your own showpiece. Make the rosy carnations in advance in royal icing—then decorating the tiers is simple. Morning Song serves 474 guests.

Accessories you'll need

Bridal couple figures, page 68
4½" Heart base, page 68
Two 10" and two 14" round separator plates, page 70
Eight 5" Grecian pillars, page 71
Four Kissing lovebirds, page 68
Arched pillar tier set, page 69
Dowel rods, page 70
Ornament (ornaments shown on pages 75-80)
Twelve 1" Filigree bells, page 68

Sunrise is decorated in the enchanting Philippine style* that everyone loves. Masses of dainty flowers, surfaces covered with quick "sotas", and a most original version of the Dowel-and-pillar construction make Sunrise unique. To prepare the separator, turn bottom 7" square plate upside down (projections down). Glue four pillars to center of plate, setting them as close together as possible. Glue tops of pillars to second 7" square plate, projections up. Pillar projection on plates will be pushed into tiers. Lower tier of Sunrise serves 72 guests.

Accessories you'll need

Curved gothic window, page 68
Petite Bridal couple, page 68
Two 7" square separator plates, page 70
Four 7" Corinthian pillars, page 71
Four Musical trio figures, page 68
(to trim pillars)

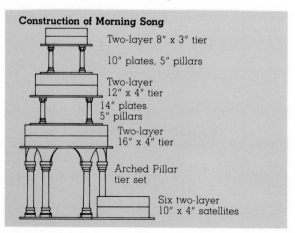

Construction of Morning Song

Two-layer 8" x 3" tier

10" plates, 5" pillars

Two-layer
12" x 4" tier

14" plates
5" pillars

Two-layer
16" x 4" tier

Arched Pillar
tier set

Six two-layer
10" x 4" satellites

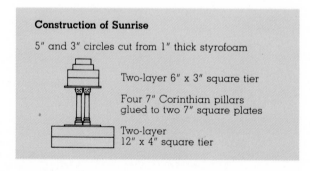

Construction of Sunrise

5" and 3" circles cut from 1" thick styrofoam

Two-layer 6" x 3" square tier

Four 7" Corinthian pillars
glued to two 7" square plates

Two-layer
12" x 4" square tier

*For a complete picture story on Philippine decorating, see *The Wilton Way of Cake Decorating,* Volume Two.

Most architectural method

STACKED CONSTRUCTION

using

SEPARATOR PLATES
BUT NO PILLARS

3

In this method the tiers rise one above the other with no interruption of pillars, very much like a set-back building. Stacked construction achieves a cake with a very strong, imposing appearance. Essentially, the stacked method is the same as the Dowel-plus-pillar construction, page 21. Follow the steps for this updated method carefully—your finished masterpiece will never shift or topple.

The cake we are illustrating uses 14", 10" and 6" round tiers. The method will be the same regardless of the number or sizes of the tiers.

1

1. Start by placing the iced 14" base tier on a prepared cake board or tray. Use a few strokes of royal icing on the board to secure. Center an 8" cake circle (one size smaller than tier above) on the tier to define a circle. Remove cake circle and insert seven dowels, cut to height of tier, (not including thickness of icing) just as shown in picture 1, page 21. Use circle as guide for even spacing.

2

2. Now the method changes from the dowel-plus-pillar construction. Press a 10" round separator plate, projections down, on the base tier, letting the pillar projections push into tier.* Make sure the plate is centered. Put strokes of royal icing on plate and set 10" tier on plate.

3. Press a small plate or saucer, 4" or 5" in diameter, on top of 10" tier to define a circle. Remove plate. Insert five evenly spaced dowels, clipped to height of tier, into tier. See page 21. Dowels should be pushed straight down to touch plate below. Now center a 6" separator plate, projections down, on tier top. Gently press so that pillar projections push into tier.

4

4. Stroke the 6" plate with royal icing and set 6" tier on it. Your cake is completely assembled and ready to decorate. Start at the top and work down.

Please note: You may choose to use a separator plate slightly smaller than the tier resting on it— that is, a 9" plate under a 10" tier. If a plate the same size as the tier is used, the base border will conceal it. The use of the separator plate below the tiers makes for a strong slip-proof construction.

For number of dowels to use for various sizes of tiers, see page 21.

Most architectural method
STACKED CONSTRUCTION

BRIDAL BELLS

Bridal Bells shows how a cake can appear like a stately little ediface when the tiers are assembled in stacked construction. Ruffled garlands, lacy bells and lavish flowers soften the severe silhouette. Construct Bridal bells just as shown on page 27. Serve three lower tiers to 340 guests.

Accessories you'll need

Top ornament (ornaments are shown on pages 75 through 80)

6", 10" and 14" round separator plates, page 70

Dowel rods, page 70

Eight 2¾", twelve 2" and eight 1" Filigree bells, page 68

Decorate Bridal Bells

Pipe royal icing roses, wild roses and tiny blue drop flowers ahead of time. Since Bridal Bells is built in stacked construction, assemble all the iced tiers with separator plates and dowel rods, then decorate—starting with the base tier.

Divide and mark all tiers for garlands. Each side of base tier is divided into fifths, 14" tier is divided into twelfths, two top tiers into sixths. Pipe shell borders on all tiers, then ruffles and curved garlands. Attach bells on base and 10" tiers in pairs, add satin ribbon bows and trim with flowers.

Construction of Bridal Bells

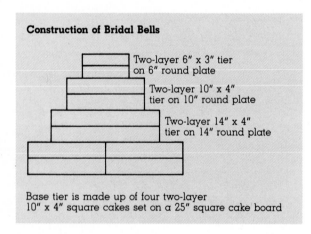

Two-layer 6" x 3" tier on 6" round plate

Two-layer 10" x 4" tier on 10" round plate

Two-layer 14" x 4" tier on 14" round plate

Base tier is made up of four two-layer 10" x 4" square cakes set on a 25" square cake board

Most architectural method
STACKED CONSTRUCTION
HEART'S DESIRE

Heart's Desire . . . a flounced confection as pretty as the bride's dress! Its architectural stacked construction (page 27) is sweetened by ruffled white petunias that accent the curving heart shapes of the tiers. Pipe all the flowers in royal icing in advance—then decorating is easy and care free. Very feminine, very impressive, Heart's Desire serves 366 reception guests.

Accessories you'll need

Top ornament
(Ornaments are shown on pages 75-80)
One 8", one 11" and one 14"
Heart separator plates*, page 70
Dowel rods, page 70
Gum paste flower accessory kit, page 67 (for non-toxic chalk for flowers)
Eight feet of Tuk-n-ruffle, page 67

Decorate Heart's Desire

Do petunias in royal icing well in advance of decorating the cake. Use tube 104 and a 2½" lily nail to pipe about 50 large flowers. Make 50 smaller flowers using tube 102 and a 1⅝" nail. After the flowers have dried, use an artist's brush and yellow chalk to tint the inside of the throats. Then add tube 16 star centers and tube 2 stamens. Pipe royal icing spikes on the backs of about half of the flowers to push into tier sides.

After assembling the tiers with dowels and separator plates, mark a curve on top of base tier following the shape of the heart tier above, but about 2" away from the heart tier. Mark two more curves, each about 2" away from the preceding one. These curves will guide three rows of ruffles. Pipe tube 17 shell borders at top and bottom of all tiers, then add big tube 126 ruffles and beading. Finish with lavish garlands of flowers and a few leaves.

*Tiers are slightly larger than separator plates

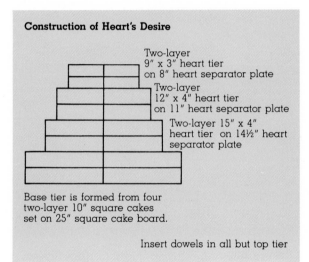

Construction of Heart's Desire

Two-layer
9" x 3" heart tier
on 8" heart separator plate
Two-layer
12" x 4" heart tier
on 11" heart separator plate
Two-layer 15" x 4"
heart tier on 14½" heart
separator plate

Base tier is formed from four
two-layer 10" square cakes
set on 25" square cake board.

Insert dowels in all but top tier

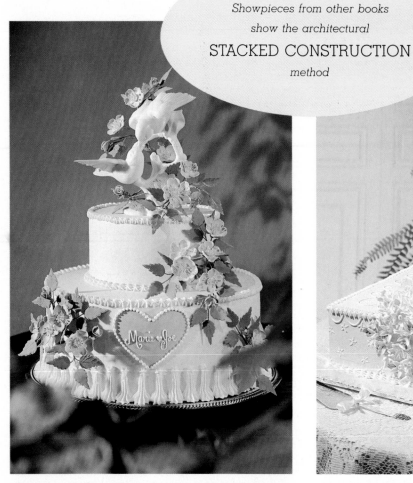

Briar Rose is the sweetest of shower cakes graced by sprays of delicate gum paste flowers. See the easy way to make them in the book that comes with the Gum paste flower kit. The heart-shaped plaque with the couple's names is gum paste, too. See construction method on page 27. Serve Briar Rose to 42 party guests.

Accessories you'll need

Gum paste flowers kit, Gum paste mix and Accessory kit, page 67
Kissing lovebirds ornament, page 68
6" round separator plate, page 70
Dowel rods, page 70

Orange Blossom. The traditional bridal flower is the trim on this wedding cake, but the assymetrical version of the stacked construction makes it look very new. All-over piped "embroidery" gives a dainty look and is set off by the pastel icing. Serve base tier of Orange Blossom to 108 wedding guests.

Accessories you'll need

Top ornament (ornaments are shown on pages 75-80)
7" square separator plate, page 70
Dowel rods, page 70

Construction of Briar Rose

Two-layer 6" x 3" tier
on 6" separator plate

Two-layer
12" x 4" tier

Construction of Orange Blossom

Two-layer 8" square tier
on 7" square separator plate

Two-layer
12" x 18" x 4" tier

Wedding beauties from other books
show the architectural
STACKED CONSTRUCTION
method

Candelight. Twinkling candles march up a flower-strewn stairway! This cake shows how dramatic a stacked cake can be. Follow the construction methods on page 27, add interesting borders, then attach Stairsteps to tiers and cover with drop flowers. Serve to 140 guests.

Accessories you'll need
Top ornament (ornaments
are shown on pages 75-80)
6" and 10" round separator plates, page 70
Stairsteps, page 68
Dowel rods, page 70

White Satin . . . a glittering, exquisite showpiece covered and trimmed with shining pulled sugar. For a complete picture lesson on how to create it, see *The Wilton Way of Cake Decorating*, Volume Two. Construction is the simple Stacked method, page 27. Serve two lower tiers of White Satin to 140 wedding guests.

Accessories you'll need
Top ornament (ornaments
are shown on page 75-80)
6" and 10" round separator plates, page 70
Dowel rods, page 70

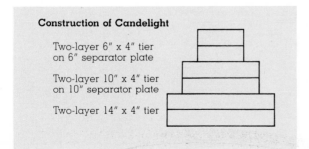

Construction of Candelight

Two-layer 6" x 4" tier
on 6" separator plate

Two-layer 10" x 4" tier
on 10" separator plate

Two-layer 14" x 4" tier

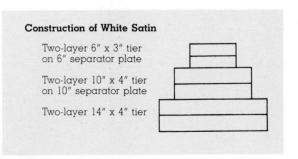

Construction of White Satin

Two-layer 6" x 3" tier
on 6" separator plate

Two-layer 10" x 4" tier
on 10" separator plate

Two-layer 14" x 4" tier

COMBINATION
STACK
and
LIFTED TIER
CONSTRUCTION

Every decorator loves this way of constructing a cake—and no wonder. It combines the imposing effect of stacked tiers with the lightness and drama that lifted tiers give the cake.

There are so many ways to achieve your masterpiece. Usually two tiers are stacked for the base, then the top tier is lifted on pillars—but you may decide to stack the two lower tiers, then lift two stacked tiers on pillars as the cake on page 45 shows. Or turn to page 41 to see three stacked tiers at the base with the two upper tiers constructed in the Push-in leg method. The combination construction gives you freedom to build unique and beautiful tier cakes.

Follow the directions for the Dowel-plus-pillar construction on page 21 for the tiers lifted on pillars. Or use the Push-in leg method, page 14. Follow the stacked construction directions, page 27 for the stacked tiers. Note that inserting dowel rods is the key to success for both.

Cherub Serenade, at right, is a very pretty example of combination construction. This sweet shower cake used the Angelic Serenade separator instead of pillars to divide the lower stacked tiers from the top tier. Decoration is quick and easy—result is a charming centerpiece for a party for the bride-to-be. Cherub Serenade serves 64 guests at a shower for the bride-to-be.

Accessories you'll need
*Party parasol, Musical trio and plate
from 3½" Heart base, page 68
Angelic serenade separator set, page 71
12" round separator plate, page 70
Dowel rods, page 70*

Decorate Cherub Serenade

This is quick because the do-it-yourself ornament, separator set and ribbon banner provide most of the trim. First make lots of drop flowers. Make a hole with a heated nail in center of Heart plate. Insert handle of parasol in hole, securing with a mound of royal icing. Attach small cupid figures. Pipe the couple's names on a 24" length of satin ribbon. Now construct the cake, stacking the two lower tiers with the 12" separator plate and dowels. Trim lower tiers with shell borders and triple string—top tier with upright shells and string. Secure the ribbon with dots of royal icing on separator set, add the flowers.

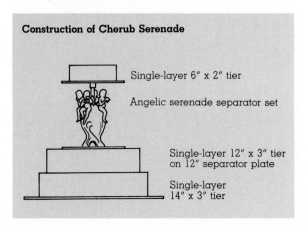

Construction of Cherub Serenade

Single-layer 6" x 2" tier

Angelic serenade separator set

Single-layer 12" x 3" tier
on 12" separator plate

Single-layer
14" x 3" tier

Most versatile method
COMBINATION CONSTRUCTION
CANDY ROSE

Candy rose . . . trim and tailored, sweet and feminine, decorated in a surprising new way! Start with tiers constructed in the versatile Combination plus-pillar method as shown on page 35. Then add broad ribbons of candy to the lower tiers and cover the top tier entirely with candy. Set it off with luscious candy roses to create a brand new dream cake for the bride! Use the candy recipe on page 65 for the trim. Serve two lower tiers of Candy Rose to 200 guests.

Accessories you'll need

Four 3" Filigree bells and top plate from
4½" Heart base, page 68 (for ornament)
Two 9" square plates and
one 11" square plate, page 70
Four 7" Corinthian pillars, page 71
Formal figures, page 68
Dowel rods, page 70
10" x 14 " doilies, page 67

Decorate Candy Rose

Make the candy recipe on page 65, then fashion the roses. You'll need about 50 to trim the tiers, separator plate and top ornament. Ice all tiers in buttercream, then assemble the two lower tiers with the 11" separator plate. Place on strong foil covered 22" cake board trimmed with doilies.

Roll out about a fourth of the remaining candy recipe into a rectangle about 32" long and ⅛" thick. Follow directions on page 65. Using a metal ruler and sharp knife, trim into two 2" strips. Gently press a strip to base of bottom tier, smoothing around corner. Press second strip to tier to complete covering the base. Do the same to the middle tier, rolling out the candy to a 25" long rectangle.

For "carpet" on separator plate, roll out a piece of the candy to a rough 9" square. Trim to a 7" square, then cut indented curves in each corner with a 2" round cutter. Place on separator plate.

Page 65 tells how to cover the top tier. To finish the cake, pipe bulb borders on all tiers, then add dropped strings. Glue bells to ornament plate, add a ribbon bow and secure a rose in each bell with icing. Secure roses to "carpeted" separator plate and lower tiers. A new masterpiece!

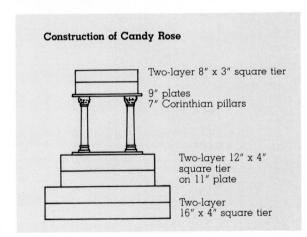

Doilies add a lacy, professional look to your foil-covered cake board. Trim off 10" x 14" rectangular doilies about 3" from the edge. Secure to cake board with dots of icing. Use only on square or rectangular boards.

Construction of Candy Rose

Two-layer 8" x 3" square tier

9" plates
7" Corinthian pillars

Two-layer 12" x 4"
square tier
on 11" plate

Two-layer
16" x 4" square tier

For information on purchasing products, please see inside front cover

38

ELEGANCE

Elegance ... a charming and refined design with subtly slanted tiers and delicate lattice trim set off by dainty flowers. Careful planning and measuring is required for its execution, but any decorator can create this outstanding confection. Build Elegance just as shown on page 34. Serve two lower tiers to 116 wedding guests.

Accessories you'll need

3" Filigree bell and plate
from 3½" Heart base, page 68, for ornament
Two 8" and one 10" round
separator plates, page 70
Four 5" Corinthian pillars, page 71
Bevel pan set, page 72
Dowel rods, page 70
Heart cookie cutters, page 73
Flower formers, page 67

Decorate Elegance

Well in advance, prepare trims. Pipe about 900 royal icing drop flowers. Mount about 50 flowers on wire stems for bouquet. For top ornament, ice a 1" thick 4" styrofoam circle with royal icing. Egg white royal icing, page 65, pipes all the separate lattice hearts. Use 1¾" heart cutters as pattern for six lattice hearts. Tape patterns to smallest Flower former, cover smoothly with wax paper and pipe the lattice and beaded edges with tube 1. Use 1¾" cutter again to pipe six hearts for side of top tier, drying over largest Flower former. Use the same cutter for six hearts that circle top of 10" tier, drying over medium Flower former. For ornament within pillars, pipe one full and two half-hearts, using 2½" cutter as pattern. Dry flat. Attach a wire to center of full heart, letting it extend below heart about 1". Assemble with half-hearts with icing.

Cover tiers with rolled fondant as directed on page 65. Assemble two lower tiers. Divide top tier into sixths to mark for garlands. Divide top of middle tier into sixths, lower part into twelfths. Do the same for bottom tier. Press the lower part of a 3" cutter into tier. Mark base bevel into sixths and mark double hearts with a 1¾" cutter.

Pipe lattice hearts on base bevel with tube 1. Do bulb borders on all tiers. To make lattice baskets on bottom tier, pipe a zigzag tube 16 garland at top of vertical surface. Overpipe three times, to form a "shelf". Pipe tube 1 lattice to marks to form basket. On 10" tier, drop triple strings at base, then string guide lines for flowers. Overpipe guidelines with tube 4.

At base of top tier pipe a bulb border. Drop a string guideline to mark garlands, dropping slightly below separator plate. Overpipe with a tube 4 zigzag. Attach styrofoam circle to top and add bulb border. Glue bell to 3½" ornament plate for vase and arrange stemmed flowers. Finally attach all lattice hearts with dots of icing. Pipe a 1" mound of icing in center of separator plate and insert wire on heart ornament. Trim cake with flowers. Elegance is complete!

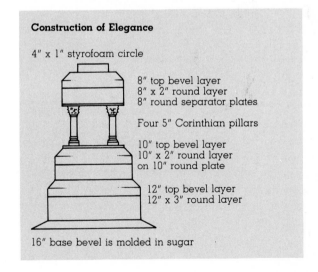

Construction of Elegance

4" x 1" styrofoam circle

8" top bevel layer
8" x 2" round layer
8" round separator plates

Four 5" Corinthian pillars

10" top bevel layer
10" x 2" round layer
on 10" round plate

12" top bevel layer
12" x 3" round layer

16" base bevel is molded in sugar

For information on purchasing products, please see inside front cover

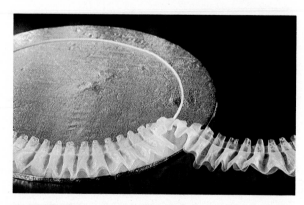

Tuk-n-Ruffle gives a frilly touch to your tier cake. To apply it, first pipe a ring of royal icing on your foil-covered cake board about 3" in from edge. Set the ruffle so the edge of the plastic lines up with the edge of the cake board. Press ruffle to secure, then attach base tier to cake board.

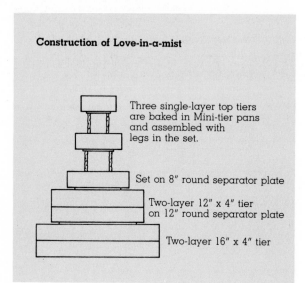

Construction of Love-in-a-mist

Three single-layer top tiers are baked in Mini-tier pans and assembled with legs in the set.

Set on 8" round separator plate

Two-layer 12" x 4" tier on 12" round separator plate

Two-layer 16" x 4" tier

Love-in-a-mist . . . as lovely as the old-fashioned flower! Daintily piped lace pieces circle the lower tiers, thread-like strings drop from the two upper tiers. Even the handmade top ornament looks like a lacy flower. This exquisite cake is an unusual example of the Combination method—the three lower tiers are stacked, just as shown on page 27, but the upper tiers are constructed in the Push-in leg method described on page 14. Study the diagram, then create your own version of this lacy masterpiece. Two lower tiers of Love-in-a-mist serve 186 wedding guests.

Accessories you'll need

Round mini-tier set, page 72
Wire from gum paste accessory kit, page 67
Six Small doves, page 68
8" and 12" round separator plates, page 70
Dowel rods, page 70
4½ feet of white Tuk-n-ruffle, page 67

Decorate Love-in-a-mist

Pipe lace pieces first with tube 1 and egg white royal icing, page 65. Use patterns on inside back cover. You will need twelve of each size for the tiers, but make extras. Pipe the pieces for the top ornament—one full and four half-hearts. Lay a 5½" length of florists' wire on the center of the full heart, about 2½" extending below it (to push into tier). Secure with a line of icing. When dry, assemble with half-hearts to create dimensional ornament. Prop with cotton balls until dry. Pipe many small drop flowers in royal icing.

The rest of the decorating is easy. Divide three lower tiers into twelfths and mark for strings and lace pieces. Pipe bulb borders on all tiers, then pipe strings. On two upper tiers, drop strings from separator plates and add scallops as picture shows. This is just as quick and easy as piping strings on the side of a tier. Secure flowers in little cascades. Add doves on tier below top. We suggest you add lace pieces, hanging strings and top ornament at the reception site. Attach lace pieces with dots of icing.

Add the sparkle of
falling water with the

KOLOR-FLO
FOUNTAIN

TURN A SIMPLE CAKE
INTO A FASCINATING SPECTACLE

Every bride loves the fountain and wants to incorporate it into her own dream cake. No wonder—the cascades are lit from below to glow softly as they fall into the basin. There are many imaginative ways to use the fountain as part of your cake design. Leaf through the following pages to see just a few. Simple operating directions come with the fountain. Just assemble your tiers with the fountain, plug it in and watch the magic begin!

Love's Garden, at right, shows how a simply decorated cake becomes a flowering vision when the fountain is its focal point. Construction is the Combination method described on page 34.* Love's Garden is spectacular, but not a large cake. The two lower tiers serve 166 guests.

Accessories you'll need

*Top ornament (ornaments are shown
on pages 75 through 80)
Flower spike, page 68
6" Heart separator plate, page 70
Three 11" Heart separator plates, page 70
Three 7" Corinthian pillars, page 71
3" Filigree bell and plate
from 3½" Heart base, page 68
Five-column tier set, page 69
Kolor-Flo fountain, page 69
Filigree fountain frame, page 69
Five Floral scroll bases, page 68
Dowel rods, page 70
Fresh flowers*

Decorate Love's Garden

Do everything with fast star tubes. To speed the work, designs on 16" round tier and 9" heart tier are imprinted with Pattern presses. Glue bell to base plate to form vase. Wedge florists' clay into bell and five bases, set upside down. Moisten the clay and arrange fresh flowers.

Add final touches on the reception table. Set fountain within tall pillars and slip filigree frame over it. Assemble tiers. Place flower filled bell within 7" pillars and insert Flower spike in 9" heart tier. Fill with water, using an eye-dropper, then arrange a few flowers in spike. Surround fountain with five flower arrangements.

It is not necessary to insert dowel rods into the 9" heart tier. The single-layer 6" heart tier above is very light.

Construction of Love's Garden

Single-layer 6" heart tier

Two-layer 9" x 3" heart tier

Three 7" pillars,
two 11" heart separator plates

Two-layer 12" x 4"
heart tier on
11" heart separator plate

Two-layer
16" x 4" round tier

Five-column tier set
Kolor-Flo fountain is set within
filigree fountain frame

Add the sparkle of falling water
USING THE KOLOR-FLO FOUNTAIN
CLASSIC ROSE

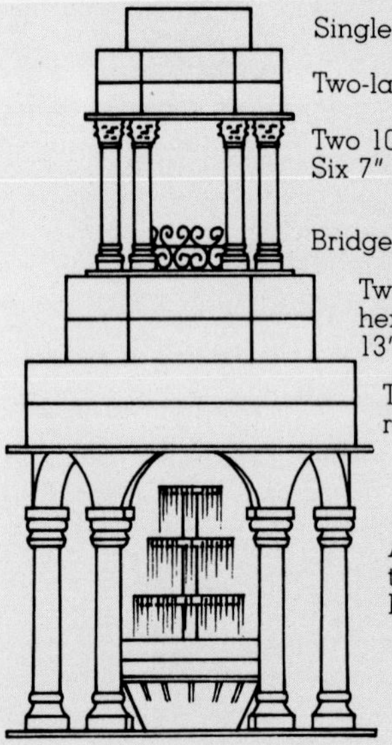

Classic Rose . . . a serenely beautiful cake inspired by the sparkling fountain. Arched pillars, designed to frame the fountain, lift the tiers. Upper hexagonal tiers echo the six-sided arrangement of pillars. Construct Classic Rose in the Combination method, page 34. Serve two lower tiers to 186 wedding guests.

Accessories you'll need
Two 10" Hexagon separator plates, page 70
Six 7" Corinthian pillars, page 71
Formal figures, page 68
Bridge from Filigree stairway set, page 74
Arched pillar tier set, page 69
Kolor-Flo fountain, page 69
Flower-holder ring, page 69
Dowel rods, page 70

Decorate Classic Rose
In advance, pipe about 160 roses and buds in various sizes. Use royal icing in pale yellow and white. For arrangement in Flower holder ring, mount about 40 roses on wire stems. Pipe about 40 leaves on wire. Wedge styrofoam into ring and arrange flowers and leaves. (See page 8.)

Assemble two lower tiers and two upper tiers* on plates. Working from top down, decorate each set of stacked tiers. Star tubes do all the shell borders, curved scrolls and strings. Mound icing on top tier and arrange roses and buds. Trim lower tiers with roses. Assemble the cake on the reception table. Set flower-filled ring on bottom plate, set fountain within it. Glue cupids to base plate, and attach flower trim to pillars with royal icing.

Construction of Classic Rose

Single-layer 6" x 2" round tier

Two-layer 9" x 3" hexagon tier

Two 10" hexagon plates
Six 7" Corinthian pillars

Bridge from stairway set

Two-layer 12" x 4"
hexagon tier on
13" hexagon plate

Two-layer 16" x 4"
round tier

Arched pillar
tier set.
Kolor-Flo fountain

*No dowel rods need be inserted in 9" hexagon tier. Single-layer 6" tier above it is very light.

46

Add the sparkle of falling water
USING THE KOLOR-FLO FOUNTAIN

CARNATION

Carnation . . . a sensational bridal cake with the surprise of a sparkling fountain at the very top! Clear fluted pillars and plates echo the fountain's radiance, the unusual trims are clusters of ruffled carnations in dainty pastels. Construct this marvelous masterpiece in the Dowel-plus-pillar method, page 21. Surround it with six satellite cakes for servings for 474 reception guests. For a smaller reception, omit the satellite cakes and serve to 186.

Construct Carnation

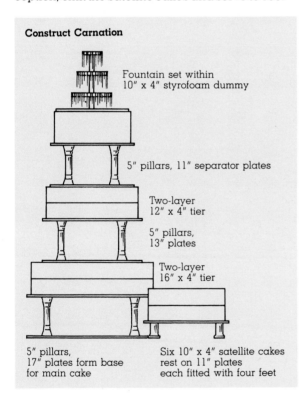

Fountain set within 10" x 4" styrofoam dummy

5" pillars, 11" separator plates

Two-layer 12" x 4" tier

5" pillars, 13" plates

Two-layer 16" x 4" tier

5" pillars, 17" plates form base for main cake

Six 10" x 4" satellite cakes rest on 11" plates each fitted with four feet

Accessories you'll need

For main cake:
   Cake leveler, page 73
   Kolor-Flo fountain, page 69
   10" x 4" round styrofoam cake dummy
   4" Filigree heart, page 68
   Crystal-look bowl, page 70
   Two 11" and two 13"
   Crystal-look plates, page 70
   Two 17" Crystal-look plates, page 69
   Twelve 5" Crystal-look pillars, page 71
   Dowel rods, page 70

For six satellite cakes:
   Six Crystal-look bowls, page 70
   Six 4" Filigree hearts, page 68
   Six 11" Crystal-look plates, page 70
   24 Crystal-look feet, page 70

Decorate Carnation

Prepare 10" dummy to hold fountain. Trace an 8" circle on top, then carve out interior with a Cake leveler, leaving a 10" ring with 1" thick walls. Cut out a small notch at base for wire of fountain. Line with foil and ice with royal icing. This dummy will be decorated just like a cake tier.

Make trims ahead. Pipe about 60 royal icing carnations with tube 150. Mount 12 on wire stems for arrangement on base tier of main cake. Curve twelve 6" lengths of florists' wire, lay on wax paper and pipe leaves for ferns with tube 65. Glue six Filigree hearts to bowls for satellite cakes. Attach wired ferns and flowers to each with royal icing. Wedge styrofoam into seventh bowl and arrange stemmed flowers and ferns.

Now decorating is fast and easy. Pipe shell borders on all tiers. For identical satellite cakes, pipe six clusters of ferns on sides. First pipe tube 3 stems, then tube 65 leaves. Add alternating double and triple strings, then a ruffly tube 67 border over shells at top. For main cake, pipe ferns and strings on all tiers, including top dummy tier. On base tier pipe tube 70 leaf borders over shells.

Assemble all tiers on the reception table. Place fountain within dummy top tier. Attach flowers with royal icing. Set prepared trims in place. Finish by piping green ferns on satellites. Isn't it lovely?

48

Add the sparkle of falling water
USING THE KOLOR-FLO FOUNTAIN

SILVER CELEBRATION

Silver Celebration . . . lacy, lofty and flower trimmed, it's a festive centerpiece for a party celebrating a 25th wedding anniversary. Lacy filigree trim veils the pillars. Construction is the Dowel-plus-pillar method, page 21, focal point is the sparkling fountain. Silver Celebration is so lovely you might want to adapt it for a wedding cake. Serve wedding-cake-sized slices to 474 guests at the anniversary party.

Accessories you'll need

Top and between-tiers ornaments, page 78
Two 7" and two 11" square
separator plates, page 70
Two 18" plates from
Arched pillar group, page 69
Fourteen Expandable pillars, page 71
20 5" and four 3" Filigree trims, page 71
Kolor-Flo fountain, page 69
Filigree fountain frame, page 69
Dowel rods, page 70
Artificial silver leaves, page 68

Decorate Silver Celebration

Pipe the royal icing roses and wild roses ahead of time. Cut a 3" x 7½" oval paper pattern and use for the rolled gum paste plaque. Do script in royal icing and tube 2. Prepare Filigree trim for two lower sets of pillars. For six pillars above base tier, glue two 5" trims together for each. For four pillars above 16" round tier, glue a 5" to a 3" trim for each. Remove top cascade from fountain.

All decoration is done with star tubes—shell borders, dropped strings, garlands and stars. Trim base tier with plaque and a curve of flowers. On the reception table, assemble the tiers. Set fountain in position and slip Filigree frame over it. Attach flowers to frame with royal icing. Secure Filigree pillar trims to separator plates with lines of icing. Complete flower trim, then trim all flowers with silver leaves.

Construction of Silver Celebration

Two-layer 6" x 4" square tier

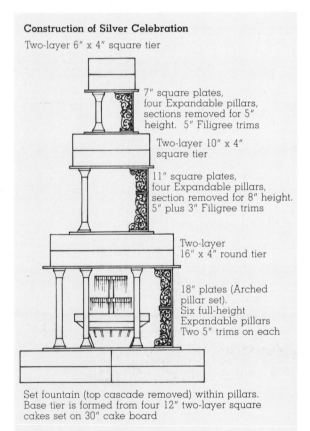

7" square plates, four Expandable pillars, sections removed for 5" height. 5" Filigree trims

Two-layer 10" x 4" square tier

11" square plates, four Expandable pillars, section removed for 8" height. 5" plus 3" Filigree trims

Two-layer 16" x 4" round tier

18" plates (Arched pillar set). Six full-height Expandable pillars Two 5" trims on each

Set fountain (top cascade removed) within pillars. Base tier is formed from four 12" two-layer square cakes set on 30" cake board

For information on purchasing products, please see inside front cover

Add the sparkle of falling water
USING THE KOLOR-FLO FOUNTAIN

BAR MITZVAH

Bar Mitzvah . . . a splendid cake of beautiful symbolism for this important occasion. Highlight of the whole scene is the sparkling fountain. Use Combination construction, page 34. Bar Mitzvah serves 60 party guests.

Accessories you'll need

Gum paste mix, page 67
(for scroll, crown and stars)
Four 5" Grecian pillars, page 71
Two 9" and one 10" round
separator plates, page 70
16 Stairsteps, page 68
Four 10½" Roman columns, page 69
Two 15" round separator plates, page 70
Kolor-Flo fountain page 69
Filigree fountain frame, page 69
Dowel rods, page 70

Decorate Bar Mitzvah

.Make rolled gum paste trims first. Using patterns on inside back cover, cut out two stars and one crown. Dry crown on 10" curve, one star on 14" curve and one star flat. Trim with royal icing. Attach Y-shaped wire to back of flat star, 2" extending below to push into tier. For scroll, cut a 12" x 3" strip of gum paste. Roll each end around a 5" pillar. Carefully check width of scroll by lining up pillars with pillar projections on plate. Dry flat, propping pillars with cotton balls.

Paint Filigree frame with thinned royal icing to match cake. Pipe royal icing bachelor buttons. Decorate tiers with star tubes, then add Stairsteps to assembled two lower tiers. Lowest stairs are 5½" from center of 14" tier. Push in pegs that come with the steps to attach. For more security, push in a peg (included with separator plates) under each step that rests against a tier. Attach curved star and crown to tiers with mounds of royal icing. Trim cake with bachelor buttons, push in star at top and add candles.

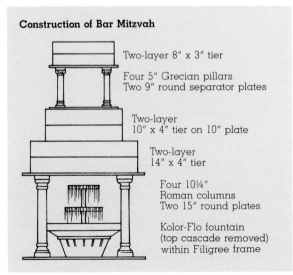

Construction of Bar Mitzvah

Two-layer 8" x 3" tier

Four 5" Grecian pillars
Two 9" round separator plates

Two-layer
10" x 4" tier on 10" plate

Two-layer
14" x 4" tier

Four 10¼"
Roman columns
Two 15" round plates

Kolor-Flo fountain
(top cascade removed)
within Filigree frame

Give instant drama and excitement

to your tier cake

ADD THE LACY

FILIGREE BRIDGE
AND STAIRWAY

It takes just a minute to transform a pretty tier cake into a lavish showpiece—just use the Filigree bridge and stairway set! Decorating is quicker, too. The bridge and stairways are so lacy and ornate that the tiers can be very simply trimmed.

For more exciting cakes using the bridge and stairway, leaf through the pages in this chapter. *Celebrate! Wedding Cakes* also shows a wonderful selection of stairway cakes.

A small cake can become much larger by adding two or more satellite cakes, and linking them to the main cake with the lacy stairways. Result is an imposing centerpiece that draws all eyes to the reception table. Another bonus—the satellite cakes are very easy to serve.

A single cake becomes a dramatic centerpiece when you add stairways. Just see how large and important the cakes on pages 52 and 55 appear. Don't save your stairways just for multiple cakes!

Large and lofty cakes, with satellites joined by the stairways, are the most marvelous of all! Add as many as six stairways—you'll create a fascinating architectural effect. The tall main cake rises like a tower from the surrounding satellites—the stairways provide the unifying elements to give a single decorative effect.

Use the bridge by itself on many cakes. It makes a dainty stage for figures, cupids, flowers or petite ornaments. Set it within pillars or on the cake top.

Advance planning is essential for bridge-and-stairway cakes to look their beautiful best. The method is easy—just relate the stairways to the height of the tiers. This page shows the method to use when the bridge is joined to the stairway. Turn the page to see how stairways are attached directly to tiers, without bridge.

Building with bridge and stairway joined

Use this method for a *main cake with a 6" top tier.* Attach the stairway to the bridge by sliding the top of the stairway into the slot beneath the bridge. Push it in as far as it will go. For a symetrical effect, push another stairway into the other side of the bridge. Stairs will hold securely.

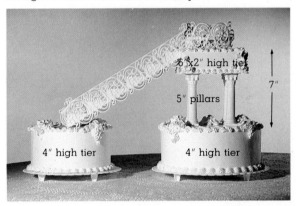

There must be a 7" difference in height of satellite cake and top of main cake as picture shows. Set main cake on reception table. Set satellite cake in approximate position at its side. Ask a helper to shift the satellite as necessary as you hold bridge and stairway *above* both cakes. Set bridge on top of main cake. Let base of stairway rest on center of satellite cake.

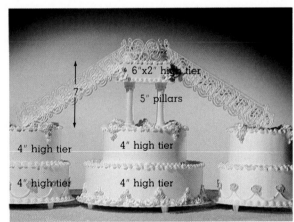

For more servings, increase heights of both main and satellite cakes. Here we have added a second satellite and stacked 4" high base tiers below all cakes. There is still a 7" difference in height between top of satellites and top of main tier.

Instant drama and excitement
USING THE FILIGREE STAIRWAY

FLOWER SHOWER

Flower shower. This graceful shower centerpiece shows how a single cake can gain beauty and importance by adding lacy stairways. Top ornament, dainty flowers and cherub musicians make it sweet enough for a petite bridal cake. The construction is Combination, page 34—two lower tiers stacked with dowels, three upper tiers built with the Push-in leg method.* Serve Flower Shower to 90 party guests.

Accessories you'll need

*Top ornament (ornaments
are shown on pages 75-80)
Round mini-tier set, page 72
Two Filigree stairways, page 74
8" round separator plate, page 73
Two 6" cake circles, page 73
Two 8" round doilies, page 67
Dowel rods, page 70
Six Musical trio figures, page 68*

Decorate Flower Shower

Make royal icing roses, daisies and drop flower forget-me-nots in advance. The rest of the decoration is very simple, very effective. Mark sides of base tier with a 10" circle to define scalloped curves, mark 9" x 13" tier with 7" and 5" circles. Do shell borders, scallops and dropped strings all with star tubes. Pictures at right show how to attach the stairways when the cake is on the reception table. Complete flower trim.

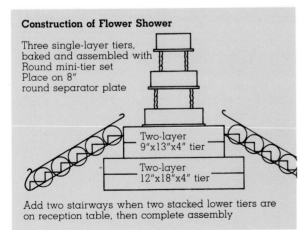

Construction of Flower Shower

Three single-layer tiers, baked and assembled with Round mini-tier set Place on 8" round separator plate

Two-layer 9"x13"x4" tier

Two-layer 12"x18"x4" tier

Add two stairways when two stacked lower tiers are on reception table, then complete assembly

*Improvise a separator plate to set below 9" x 13" tier by taping together two corrugated 9" x 13" cake boards. Wrap smoothly with plastic wrap.

Attaching stairways without bridge

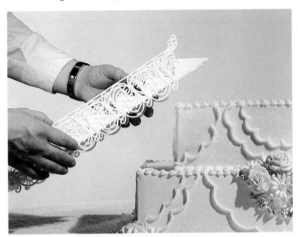

In this easy method, *allow an 8" difference in height from top to bottom of stairway,* whether base of stairway rests on table, or on a satellite cake. (In Flower Shower, each lower tier is 4" high, making a total of 8".) Set cake in position on reception table. Hold stairway above tier, top riser exactly over side of tier, triangular extension of stairway over top of tier. Push straight down. Triangular extension will sink into tier with only two strips of plastic showing on top of tier. Top riser will fit snugly against upper side of tier.

For a cake like Flower Shower, or the one on page 55, allow base of stairway to rest on table. We placed 6" cake circles covered with doilies beneath stairway bases. Conceal strips of plastic on top of tier with a few flowers. For a finishing touch, add flowers to base of stairway.

Instant drama and excitement
USING FILIGREE BRIDGE AND STAIRWAYS

STAIRWAYS TO THE STARS

Stairways to the stars. Combine square, round and heart-shaped tiers, construct them in the Combination method, page 34, trim with ruffles and sunny sweet peas. Now add four lacy stairways, each rising to the happy bridal couple. You've created an exciting wedding masterpiece guests will talk about for weeks! Serve three lower tiers of Stairways to the Stars to 226 guests.

Accessories you'll need

Cherub card holder, two Small doves and plate from 3½" Heart base, page 68 (for top ornament)
Two 8" Heart separator plates, page 70
Three 3" Grecian pillars, page 71
Two 9" round separator plates, page 70
Four 7" Corinthian pillars, page 71
Formal figures, page 68
Filigree bridge and four Filigree stairways, page 74
Twelve Musical trio cherubs, page 68
12" round separator plate, page 70
Dowel rods, page 70
Four 6" cake circles, page 73
Four 8" round doilies, page 67

Decorate Stairways to the Stars

Pipe about 300 royal icing sweet peas in advance. Pipe a tube 104 "sweet pea" border at bottom of base tier, reverse shell border at top. Use tube 104 to pipe scallops around 12" round tier, eight ruffled garlands on side and "pleated" border at top. Divide 8" tier into tenths for ruffled garlands. Pipe a top "sweet pea" border on 8" round and heart tier. Attach flowers in clusters and garlands.

Assemble on the reception table. Attach four stairways to 12" round tier, rising over center of each side of base tier. Let bases of stairways rest on doily-covered cake circles. Page 53 shows just how to do this. Now secure 9" round separator plate to top of 12" tier. It will partially cover the two strips of plastic showing on top of tier.

Complete construction of tiers. Trim stairways with flowers and bows, set cherubs on the stairs.

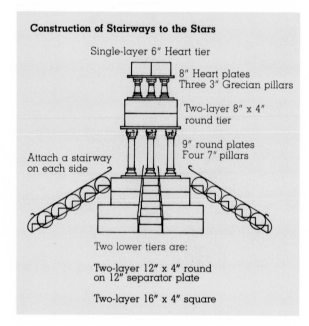

Construction of Stairways to the Stars

Single-layer 6" Heart tier

8" Heart plates
Three 3" Grecian pillars

Two-layer 8" x 4" round tier

9" round plates
Four 7" pillars

Attach a stairway on each side

Two lower tiers are:

Two-layer 12" x 4" round on 12" separator plate

Two-layer 16" x 4" square

For information on purchasing products, please see inside front cover

Instant drama and excitement
USING FILIGREE BRIDGE AND STAIRWAYS
GRAND BAROQUE

Grand Baroque . . . a magnificent centerpiece for the most formal of wedding receptions! Three stairways (one unseen here) lead from satellite cakes to the lofty main cake crowned with the bridal couple. Construction is the Combination method described on page 34. Serve to 400 guests.

Accessories you'll need
Formal figures, page 68
Filigree bridge and three
Filigree stairways, page 74
Kissing lovebirds, page 68
Two 10" and one 13" Hexagon
separator plates, Dowel rods, page 70
Six 7" Corinthian pillars, page 71
One 12" round separator plate, page 70
Nine Musical trio figures, page 68

Decorate Grand Baroque
For a rich, unified effect, paint all plastic accessories with thinned royal icing tinted ivory to match the tiers. Even the bride's figure is dressed in an ivory tulle skirt and veil. This is truly a monochromatic cake. Pipe twelve royal icing wild roses with tube 102 and 700 tiny drop flowers. Now pipe tube 20 royal icing "S" scrolls on the stairways and bridge, following filigree designs. Ice all tiers in ivory buttercream.

Piping looks elaborate, but is really very simply done. Pipe heavy tube 22 "C" scrolls and fans on all tiers, adding tube 126 fluted ruffles to some. Do shell borders. Pipe stems, attach flowers. Assemble three lower tiers of main cake, place on reception table, then secure three stairways as shown on page 53. These are placed above every other side of 15" hexagon tier. Now add 10" separator plates, pillars and top tier. Just splendid!

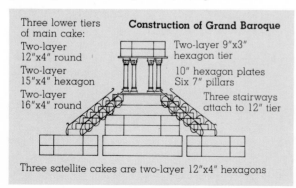

Three lower tiers of main cake:
Construction of Grand Baroque

Two-layer 12"x4" round

Two-layer 15"x4" hexagon

Two-layer 16"x4" round

Two-layer 9"x3" hexagon tier

10" hexagon plates Six 7" pillars

Three stairways attach to 12" tier

Three satellite cakes are two-layer 12"x4" hexagons

57

58

HAPPY HEARTS

Happy Hearts . . . large and important—dainty and feminine! Five lacy stairways rise over the five tall pillars at the base. Lacy filigree trims every pillar and surrounds the top tier. Quick star tubes make the decorating surprisingly easy. Make this masterpiece for a large formal wedding reception. Happy Hearts serves 466 guests.

Accessories you'll need

For main cake:

Ornaments for top and within pillars (ornaments are shown on pages 75-80)

Five Filigree stairways, page 74

Two 7" and two 11" round separator plates, page 70

Four 5" and four 7" Corinthian pillars, page 71

Five-column tier set, page 69

3" Filigree bell and plate from 3½" Heart base (for flowers within pillars), page 68

Heart bowl vase (for large floral arrangement), page 68

66 Scrolls (for pillar and ornament trim), page 68

15 Musical trio figures, Page 68

Dowel rods, page 70

Fresh flowers

For five satellite cakes:

Ten 7" round separator plates, page 70

20 3" Grecian pillars, page 71

60 Scrolls (to trim pillars), page 68

Dowel rods, page 70

Decorate Happy Hearts

Trim all tiers with quick star tubes. Glue bell to Heart base plate, wedge in florist's clay, moisten and arrange a few flowers. Make large arrangement in Heart bowl vase. Assemble satellite cakes and base tier of main cake on the reception table. Add five stairways (page 53), then complete assembly of main cake. Attach Scrolls to pillars with dots of royal icing. Position ornaments and flower arrangements. Add cupid figures on stairs. Spectacular!

Construction of Happy Hearts

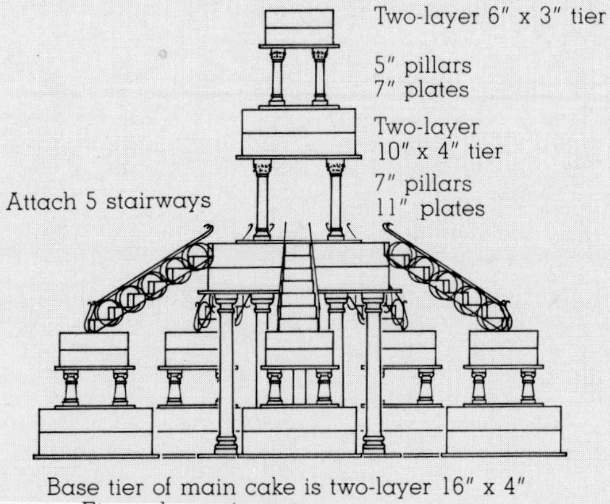

Two-layer 6" x 3" tier

5" pillars
7" plates

Two-layer
10" x 4" tier

7" pillars
11" plates

Attach 5 stairways

Base tier of main cake is two-layer 16" x 4" on Five-column tier set

Five 2-tier satellite cakes
Top tiers are two-layer 6" x 3"
3" pillars, 7" plates
Base tiers are two-layer 10" x 4"

For information on purchasing products, please see inside front cover

Instant drama and excitement
USING FILIGREE BRIDGE AND STAIRWAYS

CRESCENDO

Crescendo, an extravagantly beautiful wedding cake! The main cake rises like a sculptured tower above six satellite cakes joined by lacy stairways. A fountain sparkles within tall Arched pillars. The Dowel-plus-pillars method, page 21, is used for construction, stairways are attached as shown on page 53. Serve Crescendo to 474 reception guests.

Accessories you'll need

For Main cake:
> Top ornament (ornaments are shown on pages 75-80)
> Two 9" and two 13" round separator plates, page 70
> Six 5" and six 7" Corinthian pillars, page 71
> Twelve stud plates, page 71
> 4¼" Heart base, page 68
> Six Angelinos, page 68
> Filigree bridge, page 74
> Formal figures, page 68
> Arched pillar tier set, page 69
> Kolor-Flo fountain, page 69
> Filigree fountain frame, page 69

For six satellite cakes:
> Six Lazy daisy servers, page 74
> Six Filigree stairways, page 74
> Formal figures, six men, six girls, page 68

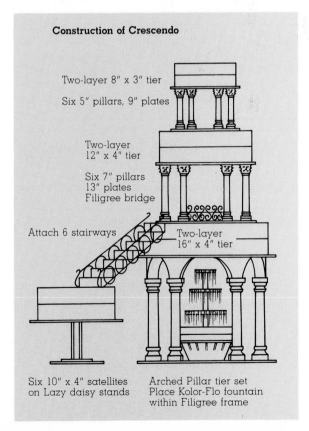

Construction of Crescendo

Two-layer 8" x 3" tier

Six 5" pillars, 9" plates

Two-layer 12" x 4" tier

Six 7" pillars 13" plates Filigree bridge

Attach 6 stairways

Two-layer 16" x 4" tier

Six 10" x 4" satellites on Lazy daisy stands

Arched Pillar tier set Place Kolor-Flo fountain within Filigree frame

For decorating directions, please turn the page

Dressing the girl's Formal Figure

You can turn this figurine into almost any personality you want—a bride, a bridesmaid, a graduate, "sweet sixteen" or a lady celebrating an anniversary. It's more fun than dressing a doll!

1. To follow the color scheme of the reception or party, paint the dress. Wash the figure in sudsy water to make sure it is grease-free. Tint about a half-cup of royal icing to the shade you desire. Stir in a tablespoon of water, then, if necessary, add more water, drop by drop, until the icing has the consistency of cream. This amount will cover six or more figures. Use a small artist's brush to paint the dress. Let dry and give a second coat if needed.

2. Add a nylon tulle skirt. (Tulle is available at most fabric shops.) Fold a 7" x 14" piece of tulle in half for a 7" square. Cut out a 6" double circle. Fold in quarters and cut off about ¼" from the point. Cut a small wedge out of circle from outer edge to center waistline hole. Attach skirt to figure by running a thread around waistline of skirt. Knot at back, letting opening slightly overlap.

3. Set figure on a styrofoam block and pin down folds. Spray with clear acrylic to hold folds. Dry.

4. Trim the bodice and skirt with tiny ruffles, dots and scallops as you desire, using tube 00L or 000 and royal icing. Pipe tiny drop flowers and attach to hands with dots of icing. Add streamers of ⅛" satin ribbon.

5. For a bridal veil, cut a tulle rectangle 4½" x 8½". Round the corners. Fold in half to 4½" x 4¼". Gather along fold to bring to about ½". Attach gathered edge to head with dots of royal icing. Spray with clear acrylic to hold folds. Add royal icing drop flowers and "embroidered lace" edges.

Crescendo, continued

Decorate Crescendo

This is a large and elaborate cake, but by making trims ahead, final decorating is easy.

Pipe about 320 royal icing wild roses with tubes 101 and 103. Mount 20 on florists' wire stems and pipe leaves on wire. Wedge styrofoam into the Heart base and arrange a bouquet for between-tiers. Prepare the two sets of separator plates to receive six pillars. With a pliars, snap off two opposite pillar projections on each plate.

Now glue on four stud plates, making sure they are evenly spaced. Dress the bride and bridesmaid figures in tulle skirts. Add bouquets.

Decorate identical satellite cakes. Divide sides into tenths and drop tube 13 string. Add shell borders, scallop trim on top and flowers.

On main cake, divide base tier into 18ths, middle tier into 6ths and top tier into 12ths. Do all piping with star tubes. Attach Angelinos to middle tier on mounds of icing.

Assemble base tier of main cake on the reception table. Arrange satellite cakes and attach stairways as shown on page 53. Complete assembly, then add flower and ribbon trim. Pose figures on bridge and stairway.

How to make decorating tier cakes easier and faster

Overcome your fears! If you are new to decorating tier cakes, just remember they are only groups of smaller cakes put together. Each of them is really easier to decorate than a small cake. Construction and accessories go a long way in the final appearance, so trims may be simple.

Assemble tiers completely before decorating. (An exception: cakes constructed in the Push-in Leg method.) This gives you a chance to judge the overall effect of the cake and decide on tubes to use. At this time, mark center back and front of each tier. If measuring and marking is necessary, do it now, so trims will line up. Some master decorators even decorate the tiers while they are assembled—achieving a very unified effect. Of course, you may take tiers apart to decorate after they have been marked.

Separator plates won't stick to the icing on tier tops, if you sprinkle a little shredded coconut over the area where the plate will be placed. Or sift confectioners' sugar, using a small sieve. Plates will lift off easily when you are ready to serve the cake. Remember this when you assemble stacked tiers, or tiers constructed with the Dowel-and-pillar method.

Decorate base tier first, then work your way from the largest to smallest tier. For most designs, start with the bottom border and work up through side trim to top border and any piping on tier top. Exceptions are cakes in stacked construction. When tiers are completely assembled, start decorating at the top tier and work down to base tier. There'll be no danger of accidentally damaging trim on upper tiers as you pipe.

Always edge lower separator plates on cakes in Dowel-and-pillar construction with simple scallops or shells. This gives a neat finish to the tiers.

Keep your work at eye level. Only by doing this will stringwork drop in even curves, garlands be identical. If necessary, set your turntable on a strong carton, or pile of books.

Plan ahead. After you've decided on the design of your cake, make a list of flowers and other trims that can be piped separately, off the cake. Pipe these in royal icing, weeks or even months ahead. Then decorating the tiers is easy and fun.

Take a "survival kit" to the reception site. Include a sealed container of icing, parchment triangles for making cones, a few tubes. Scissors, needle and thread and extra flowers are also handy. Then it's easy to make small repairs in a hurry.

How to carry a tier cake to the reception or party room

Use this method for safe transportation of your masterpieces—even for hundreds of miles.

For cakes constructed in Center Column, Push-in Leg or Dowel-and-Pillar methods.

1. Make tracings of the cake board or separator plates on which the tiers rest. Transfer to large pieces of soft foam, 3" or 4" thick. Following the tracings, use a sharp knife to cut out depressions ½" deep for each tier.

2. If you are using a car, you will need a plywood platform to level the back seat. Place the pieces of foam on the platform, or on the floor of a station wagon or van. Take tiers apart if constructed in Center Column or Push-in Leg method. *Leave columns or legs in place.* Remove pillars from Dowel-and-Pillar cakes. Place the tiers carefully in the depressions in the foam. Assemble on the reception table.

3. To protect from dust, cover the tiers with lightweight plastic (cleaner's bags are fine). Keep the tiers out of direct sunlight.

For Stacked or Combination cakes

For a stacked cake, use the same method of transportation, but set the entire assembled cake into a foam depression.

For a combination cake, take tiers apart, keeping stacked tiers as units. Then set tiers into depressions cut in soft foam.

Save the pieces of soft foam for future cakes.

Party cake serving chart

Use this chart for estimating servings for shower cakes, birthday cakes or any cake for a party. These are two-layer, dessert-size portions.

For estimating servings for wedding cakes, see chart on page 66.

SHAPE	SIZE	SERVINGS	SHAPE	SIZE	SERVINGS
ROUND	6"	6	HEART	6"	6
	8"	10		9"	12
	10"	14		12"	24
	12"	22		15"	35
	14"	36			
			HEXAGON	6"	6
SQUARE	6"	8		9"	12
	8"	12		12"	20
	10"	20		15"	48
	12"	36			
	14"	42	PETAL	6"	6
				9"	8
REC-	9"x13"	24		12"	26
TANGLE	11"x15"	35		15"	48
	12"x18"	54			

TESTED RECIPES

Wilton snow-white buttercream

Very easy to use for covering tiers and stays soft and toothsome. Borders hold their shape well. Use it also for cake-top flowers. Use a heavy-duty, stationary mixer.

⅔ cup water

4 tablespoons meringue powder

1¼ cups solid white shortening

11½ cups confectioners' sugar, sifted

¾ teaspoon salt

¼ teaspoon butter flavoring

½ teaspoon almond flavoring

½ teaspoon clear vanilla flavoring

Combine water and meringue powder in large mixer bowl and whip at high speeds until peaks form. Add four cups sugar, one cup at a time, beating after each addition at low speed.

Alternately add shortening and remainder of sugar. Add salt and flavorings and beat at low speed until smooth. May be stored, well covered, in refrigerator for several weeks. Bring to room temperature to rebeat. Yield: eight cups. Recipe may be cut in half or doubled.

Chocolate buttercream

A delicious variation! Blend in a mixture of 1 cup of cocoa and four tablespoons of water to the recipe above before adding shortening.

Wilton boiled icing—egg white

Fine for covering tiers. Do not use for borders or flowers. Keep all utensils grease-free.

Mixture one:

2 cups granulated sugar

½ cup water

¼ teaspoon cream of tartar

Mixture Two:

4 egg whites, room temperature

1½ cups confectioners' sugar, sifted

Combine granulated sugar, water and cream of tartar in a 1½-quart heavy saucepan. Place over high heat and stir until all sugar crystals are dissolved. Wash down sides of pan with a pastry brush dipped in hot water. After this, do not stir. At 240°F. remove from heat.

Meanwhile, whip egg whites seven minutes at high speed. Add hot syrup (Mixture One) slowly, beat three minutes at high speed. Turn to second speed, gradually add confectioners' sugar, beat seven minutes more at high speed. Use at once, rebeating will not restore texture. Yield: 3½ cups.

Wilton boiled icing—meringue

Many experienced decorators ice the tiers in buttercream, then use this icing for borders and trim. Pipes very easily. Be sure to have all utensils grease-free when making this recipe. Stiffen the icing with additional confectioners' sugar for piping flowers. Not for tiers.

Mixture One:

2 cups granulated sugar

½ cup warm water

¼ teaspoon cream of tartar

Mixture Two:

½ cup warm water

4 tablespoons meringue powder

3½ cups sifted confectioners' sugar

Combine ingredients in Mixture One in a 1½ quart heavy saucepan. Place over high heat and stir until all sugar crystals are dissolved. After this, do not stir. Insert candy thermometer and wash down sides of pan with a pastry brush dipped in hot water. At 240°F, remove from heat.

Meanwhile, prepare Mixture Two. Whip meringue powder and water about seven minutes or until fluffy. Add confectioners' sugar and whip at low speed about three minutes. Slowly pour hot syrup (Mixture One) into batch and whip at high speed until light and very fluffy. Use immediately or refrigerate in a tightly closed container for weeks. Bring to room temperature and rebeat to use again. Yield: 6 cups.

Wilton quick poured fondant

This icing gives a beautiful shiny surface to tiers.

4½ ounces water

2 tablespoons white corn syrup

6 cups confectioners' sugar, sifted

1 teaspoon almond flavoring

Mix water, sugar and corn syrup in a saucepan. Stir over low heat to 92°F, just lukewarm. Do not overheat. Stir in flavoring. Will cover two 10" round tiers. Recipe may be doubled or tripled.

To cover a tier with fondant, first ice smoothly with buttercream and let icing crust about an hour. Place tier on cooling rack with a cookie sheet beneath it. Pour fondant over iced tier, flowing from center and moving out in a circular motion. Touch up sides with a spatula. Excess fondant can be stored, tightly covered, in refrigerator for weeks. Reheat to use again.

Chocolate poured fondant

Follow the recipe above, but increase water to 5½ ounces. After heating, stir in 3 ounces of unsweetened melted chocolate. Delicious!

Wilton royal icing—meringue

This is the very best icing for piping flowers. Make them weeks or months ahead of time—and store in a cool dark place. Dries too hard for covering the cake. Make sure utensils are grease-free.

3 level tablespoons meringue powder
3½ ounces warm water
1 pound confectioners' sugar, sifted
½ teaspoon cream of tartar

Combine ingredients, mixing slowly, then beat at high speed for seven to ten minutes. Keep covered with a damp cloth, icing dries quickly. Store, tightly covered, in refrigerator for weeks. Bring to room temperature and rebeat to use. Yield: 3½ cups.

Wilton royal icing—egg white

This is an even stronger icing than the one above. Use it for piping lace pieces or delicate lattice. Use at once, rebeating will not restore texture. Keep utensils grease-free.

3 egg whites, room temperature
1 pound confectioners' sugar, sifted
½ teaspoon cream of tartar

Combine ingredients, beat at high speed seven to ten minutes. Dries quickly—keep covered with a damp cloth while using. Yield: 3 cups.

Rolled fondant

This is the rolled icing that gives a perfectly smooth decorating surface. Easy to use!

½ ounce unflavored gelatin
¼ cup water
2 tablespoons solid white shortening
½ cup gloucose
¾ ounce glycerine
2 lb. confectioners' sugar, sieved 3 times
2 or 3 drops clear flavoring

Put gelatin and water in a small pan and heat gently until just dissolved. Add shortening, glucose and glycerine and beat until shortening is just melted. Mix well. Put sieved sugar in a large bowl and make a well in the center. Pour warm liquid mixture into well and mix with your hands to a dough-like consistency. Transfer to a smooth surface covered with non-stick pan release and lightly dusted with cornstarch. Knead until smooth and pliable. Add flavoring while kneading. If too stiff, add a few drops of boiling water.

Use immediately or store in an airtight container at room temperature for up to a week. Knead again before rolling out. If storing longer, refrigerate and bring to room temperature before kneading. Covers an 8" x 3" square or a 9" x 3" round cake. Recipe may be doubled.

To cover a tier in rolled fondant, first ice with buttercream. Roll out fondant to about ¼" thickness. Dust your rolling pin and work surface with cornstarch. Drape fondant over tier and smooth with your hands, starting at top. Trim at base. Use a firm pound cake or fruit cake recipe for the cake.

Candy for flowers and covering tiers

Use this recipe for the exciting cake on page 36. It's so easy to smooth over a tier and fashion flowers. Make the recipe a day in advance. Mix it twice—do not attempt to double it, it would be too difficult to knead. Measure quantities carefully.

1 pound white Candy melts™ confectionery coating
3 drops Candy color
6 drops Candy flavoring
6 ounces glucose, by weight

Heat water in the bottom pan of a double boiler to simmering. Remove from heat, put top pan in position and fill with Candy melts™. Stir constantly until melted. Stir in color and flavoring. Heat the glucose until just warm and stir it into the melted coating until mixture becomes thick and forms a ball. Now knead and stretch just like taffy for about eight minutes to squeeze out the excess oil. Do this over a pan to catch the oil. Wrap in plastic wrap.

Repeat the recipe. Turn out both batches on the counter and knead to combine. Wrap tightly in plastic wrap, put in covered container and allow to rest overnight at room temperature. More than enough for the cake on page 36. Wrap tightly in plastic wrap to store at room temperature for several weeks. Knead to use again.

To cover tier, spray work surface with non-stick pan release, dust lightly with cornstarch. Knead mixture again and roll out to an area large enough to cover entire cake, about ³/₁₆" thick. Drape over rolling pin and transfer to cake. Now smooth the candy over the cake with your hands, starting at top center. The mixture remains so pliable you will have no trouble in smoothing it over the edges and corners. If a tear appears, simply patch with more candy and smooth. Trim off at base, smooth and trim again.

To make roses, read directions on page 14 of *Wilton celebrates the Rose.* Easy and fun!

Wilton gum paste mix

This magic mix makes a flexible, pliable substances that can be rolled out like pie dough, molded into charming figures or fashioned into flowers.

Combine one pound of mix and ¼ cup of water in a large bowl. Stir until well mixed. Dust your work surface with confectioners' sugar, turn our mixture on surface and knead like bread dough until mix is well worked in. Place in a tightly sealed plastic bag and let rest for 15 minutes at room temperature. Now knead again. Turn out on surface lightly dusted with confectioners' sugar. Knead for five minutes, gradually working in ⅓ cup of confectioners' sugar. Mixture should be smooth and non-sticky. Use at once, or store at room temperature in a tightly sealed plastic bag for up to six weeks. Makes hundreds of flowers.

HOW TO CUT A WEDDING CAKE

Wedding cake slices are usually 1" wide, 2" deep and two layers high. Since almost all brides like to freeze the top tier for the first anniversary, remove it first. Have a doily-covered cake circle and cake box ready.

For Stacked cakes, do not take tiers apart. Simply start at the top and work down the tiers. When you finish cutting one tier, remove the separator plate below it and slice the tier below. Follow the diagrams for method of cutting.

For Dowel-and-pillar cakes, remove the top tier, on its separator plate, from its pillars, then slice as diagrams show. Remove pillars and separator plate from tier below. Remove tier, on its plate, from pillars and slice. Continue with each upper tier. Slice base tier last.

Push-in leg cakes are cut in a similar way. After you have removed and sliced the top tier, pull out the legs from the next tier down, remove the tier, on its plate, and slice. Continue, cutting base tier last.

For Center column cakes, lift off the top tier, on its plate, and place on a smaller cake pan to steady. Cover the pan with a damp napkin so the tier will not slip. Remove the column from the tier below, then proceed, just as you did for top tier. Work down, cutting base tier last.

For Combination cakes, cut the stacked tiers as described above. Cut lifted tiers in the method described for Dowel-and-pillar or Push-in leg cakes.

Wedding cake serving chart

Here are the approximate number of 1" x 2" slices each tier will provide. All tiers are two-layer. Remember—the top tier is usually saved for the bride, so do not include it in the total servings of a cake.

SHAPE	SIZE	SERVINGS
ROUND	6"	16
	8"	30
	10"	48
	12"	68
	14"	92
	16"	118
	18"	148
SQUARE	6"	18
	8"	32
	10"	50
	12"	72
	14"	98
	16"	128
	18"	162
HEXAGON	6"	6
	9"	22
	12"	50
	15"	66
PETAL	6"	8
	9"	20
	12"	44
	15"	62
HEART	6"	12
	9"	28
	12"	48
	15"	90
RECTANGLE	9"x13"	54
	11"x15"	77
	12"x18"	108

WEDDING CAKE CUTTING CHARTS

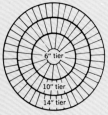

Top view of a 3-tiered round cake

To cut a round tier, move in 2" from outer edge and cut a circle. Cut 1" wide slices within it. Continue until entire tier is cut.

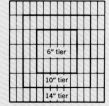

Top view of a 3-tiered square cake

To cut a square tier, move in 2" from one outer edge and cut straight across. Cut into 1" pieces. Continue until entire tier is cut. **Cut rectangular tiers** the same way.

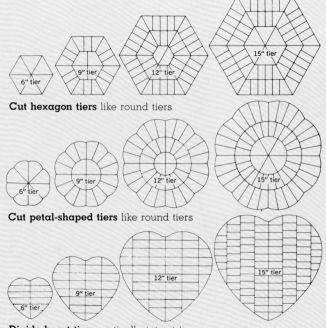

Cut hexagon tiers like round tiers

Cut petal-shaped tiers like round tiers

Divide heart tiers vertically into strips approximately 2" wide. Slice 1" pieces.

Dial divider for marking exact center of cake, dividing into fourths, quarters, sixteenths. Sturdy white plastic.
409-M-8607

Here's everything you need to create the tier cakes in this book!

For your convenience, these blue pages show all the merchandise you'll need for the cakes in this book and many more. Browse through to find the pans that form the basic shapes, all the pillars and plates that support the tiers, decorative little touches and handy time-savers. There's also a section showing the beautiful top ornaments that crown your masterpieces.

For information on purchasing products, please see inside front cover

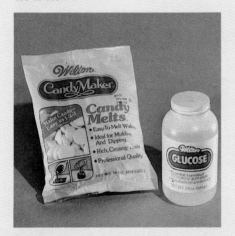

Candy Melts™ brand confectionery coating. Use in recipes, page 65, to cover tiers, make dainty flowers. Great for candy making, too. White.
1911-M-498. One-lb. bag

Glucose, needed for candy recipe for flowers and covering tiers.
707-M-109. 24-oz. jar

Fanci-foil for covering cake boards. Grease-resistant, non-toxic. Pretty pastel colors. Each roll is 20" x 15' long.

804-M-124. Rose
804-M-183. Gold
804-M-167. Silver
804-M-140. Blue
804-M-191. White

Doilies add a dainty look to any cake. Cut strips from rectangular doilies to edge cake boards, make flaps for candy boxes. All with open-work edges.

2104-M-1605. Pack of six, 10" x 14"
2104-M-1397. 8" rnd, pack of 10
2104-M-1532. 10" rnd, pack of 8
2104-M-1591. 12" rnd, pack of 6

Gum paste flowers kit. New, quick, easiest way to make exquisite flowers. Use as outstanding cake trims, arrange into centerpieces. Big full-color book shows actual-size steps. Also 24 plastic cutters, leaf mold, three wooden tools and two foam squares for quick, easy modeling.
1907-M-117. 30-piece set

Gum paste mix. (Not shown.) Add water and knead! In minutes a pliable mixture to form into flowers. Keeps for weeks. One can makes hundreds of flowers.
707-M-124. One-lb. can

Tuk-n-Ruffle to edge cake boards. Plastic ruffle with tulle overlay.

	per foot	per 60' bolt
Pink	801-M-708	802-M-702
Blue	801-M-200	802-M-206
White	801-M-1003	802-M-1008

Accessory kit. Green florist tape, fine florist wire for stems, non-toxic chalk and stamens to complete flowers.
1907-M-227. Complete kit

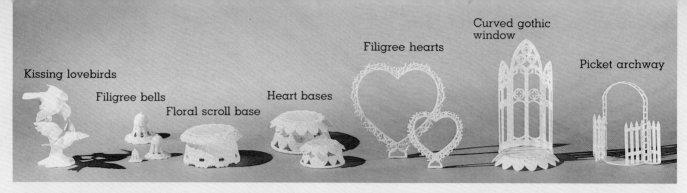

Sweet touches add charm and personality to tier cakes

All are in washable pure white plastic (unless otherwise noted).

TOP PANEL

Kissing lovebirds. Beautifully detailed to add a romantic touch between tiers or on cake top.
1002-M-206. 5½" high

Filigree bells in open-work design.
1001-M-9446. 1", pack of 12
1001-M-9421. 2", pack of 6
1001-M-9438. 2¾", pack of 6
1001-M-9403. 3", pack of 3

Floral scroll base. Lavish baroque design to hold couples or cupids. Use also as bowl for flowers. 4½" diameter.
201-M-303. Two pieces.

Heart bases. lacy heart-and-circle pattern. Each comes in two pieces.
201-M-7331. 4¼" diameter
201-M-7846. 3½" diameter

Filigree hearts. Lacy edges. Use as backgrounds for figures or cupids.
205-M-1500. 7" high, pack of 3
205-M-1528. 4" high, pack of 6

Curved gothic window. Lovely setting for couples, cupids. Two pieces.
205-M-3059. 9" high

Picket archway. Gives a garden look to a cake. Movable side fences.
205-M-343. 5½" high

MIDDLE PANEL

Old-fashioned fence. 12 posts, 12 pegs, 144 snap-together links. See "Sunny Morning" cake on page 10.
1107-M-8326. Posts 1½" high

Flower spikes. Push into cake, fill with water, using eye dropper, add flowers. They'll stay fresh for hours. 3" high
1008-M-408. Pack of 12

Artificial leaves for anniversary cakes. 144 leaves in each pack.
1005-M-6518. Gold, 1⅞"
1005-M-6712. Gold, 1¼"
1005-M-6526. Silver, 1⅞"
1005-M-6720. Silver, 1¼"

Scrolls. Give lacy effect. 2¾" high.
1004-M-2800. Pack of 24

Party parasols. Pretty for shower cakes. 4" diameter, 5" snap-on handles.
2110-M-9296. Pack of four

Small doves. Fluttery trim! 2" wide.
1002-M-1709. Pack of twelve

Push-in candle holders. Twelve pegs to push in cake plus twelve holders.
1107-M-8131 set

Stairsteps. 24 each steps, pegs, candle holders. Climbs cake side. Pegs secure steps to cake.
1107-M-8180

BOTTOM PANEL

Formal figures. Handpainted porcelain. Use for weddings, graduations, anniversaries. Pose on stairways or bases. Approximately 4¼" high.
202-M-225. Girls' figure
202-M-221. Man, white coat
202-M-223. Man, black coat

Bridal couple. Tulle veil and skirt. Standard couple, 4½" tall.
202-M-8121 White coat
202-M-8110. Black coat
Petite couple, 3½" tall.
203-M-8220. White coat
2102-M-820. Black coat

Anniversary couple. 3½" tall.
203-M-2827. Silver, 25th
203-M-1820. Gold, 50th

Musical trio. Sweet cherub band.
1001-M-368. Set of three

Angel fountain. Dainty trim.
1001-M-406. 3¾" high

Cherub card holder. Insert card or use on cake. 3⅜" high.
1001-M-9373. Set of four

Frolicking cherub. Happy touch!
1001-M-244. 5" high

Angelino. Side trim, 3" wide.
1001-M-503. Pack of six

Heart bowl vase, 5" x 3½" high.
1008-M-9685. Heart design

Kolor-Flo fountain sparkles within tall pillars

Kolor-Flo fountain turns a tier cake into an enchanting vision! Water falls from three cascades into a clear bowl lit from below. Plug in 65″ cord and the magic begins. Clear plastic bowl 9¾″ in diameter, 110-124v. A.C. motor. 11½″ overall height. Two top cascades may be removed. Directions and replacement part information.
306-M-2599. Kolor-Flo fountain

Arched Pillar Tier set, most dramatic way to frame the fountain—or a flower arrangement, or ornament. Set includes six 13″ pillars, two 18″ plates with graceful curved edges and six cherubs, all in strong snow-white plastic.
301-M-9752. Complete set
302-M-504. 18″ plate
301-M-9809. Pack of 6 pillars
303-M-9719. 13″ pillar

New Crystal-look Fountain Cascade set adds drama (at left)
Now you can transform your Kolor-Flo Fountain into an even more beautiful decorative accessory. Slip the collar over the rim of the bowl, position the three cascades and prepare to experience a moment of magic when the shimmering water begins to cascade in

Crystal-look tier set, most sparkling way to frame the fountain. Faceted cuts in strong clear plastic glitter like cut glass. Add smaller Crystal-look pillars and plates to tiers above. Set includes two 17″ plates and four 13¾″ pillars. See cake on page 47.
301-M-1387. Complete 6-pc. set
302-M-1810. 17″ plate
303-M-2242. 13¾″ pillar

sparkling rivulets. The whole fountain takes on the elegant look of cut glass! Set includes four pieces: 11½″ collar and 2½″, 4½″ and 8 inch cascades. Assembly instructions included.
306-M-1172. Four-piece set

Five-column tier set frames the fountain in classic simplicity. Five 13¾″ pillars harmonize with Grecian pillars for tiers above. Two 18″ plates are strongly reinforced, have dainty scalloped edges. Strong white plastic.
301-M-1980. Save! 7-pc. set
303-M-2129. 13¾″ pillar
302-M-1225. 18″ plate

Tall pillars for fountain

Lacy-look square pillars. White plastic. Use 14″, 15″ or 16″ round plates.
303-M-8976. 12″ high

Roman columns. Remove top cascade. Use 14″, 15″ or 16″ round plates. In strong white plastic.
303-M-8135. 10¼″ high

Flower Holder Ring fits around fountain, conceals motor. Add fresh or fabric flowers. 12¼″ diameter, 2″ high.
305-M-435. White plastic

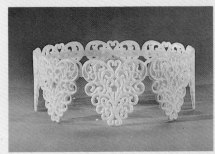

Filigree Fountain Frame snaps together, conceals motor, gives a lacy look. 3½″ x 9″ diameter.
205-M-1285. White plastic

For information on purchasing products, please see inside front cover

Separator plates in sturdy plastic...fit all Wilton pillars

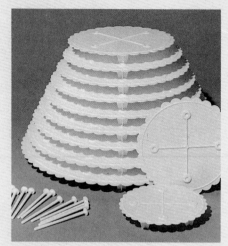

Classic round plates in eleven inch-by-inch sizes—from 6" to 16"! Strongly crafted to hold the heaviest tiers. Each includes four plastic pegs.

302-M-67. 6" plate
302-M-1306. 7" plate
302-M-83. 8" plate
302-M-1322. 9" plate
302-M-105. 10" plate
302-M-1349. 11" plate
302-M-120. 12" plate
302-M-1365. 13" plate
302-M-148. 14" plate
302-M-1403. 15" plate
302-M-946. 16" plate

Save! Buy round plate-pillar sets
Each set includes two plates, four pillars, four plastic pegs.

2103-M-639. 6" plates, 3" pillars
2103-M-925. 7" plates, 3" pillars
2103-M-256. 8" plates, 5" pillars
2103-M-912. 9" plates, 5" pillars
2103-M-108. 10" plates, 5" pillars

2103-M-939. 11" plates, 5" pillars

2103-M-124. 12" plates, 5" pillars

2103-M-955. 13" plates, 5" pillars

Save! Buy 54-pc round set
Versatile set includes two each of 6", 8",, 10", 12" and 14" plates plus 20 Grecian pillars, 5" height, 24 pegs. Create a towering 6-tier cake, or keep on hand for other cakes.
301-M-8380. 54-pc round set

Versatile square plates for easy-to-serve tiers. Reinforced snow-white plastic. Each includes four plastic pegs.
302-M-1004. 7" plate
302-M-1020. 9" plate
302-M-1047. 11" plate
302-M-1063. 13" plate

Save! Buy 30-pc. square set
Handy set includes two each of 7", 9" and 11" square plates, 12 pegs and twelve 5" Grecian pillars. Enough to build an impressive 4-tier cake or mix with other plates and pillars.
301-M-1158. Complete 30-piece set

Heart plates support romantic tiers for wedding, shower or Valentine cakes. Use heart-shaped pans to bake tiers. Four sizes—each takes three pillars. Each includes 3 pegs.
302-M-2112. 8" plate
302-M-2114. 11" plate
302-M-2116. 14½" plate
302-M-2118. 16½" plate

Crystal-look plates have pretty fluted edges, look just like cut glass, but are strong, light-weight clear plastic. Each includes four plastic pegs.

302-M-2013. 7" plates
302-M-2035. 9" plates
302-M-2051. 11" plates
302-M-2078. 13" plates

Crystal-look bowl to fill with flowers.
205-M-1404

Crystal-look feet snap on any plate.
305-M-613. Set of four feet

Hexagon plates for easy-to-decorate six-sided tiers. Match up with Hexagon pans—create a memorable tier cake. Plates require six pillars. Each includes six plastic pegs.
302-M-1705. 7" plate
302-M-1748. 10" plate
302-M-1764. 13" plate
302-M-1799. 16" plate

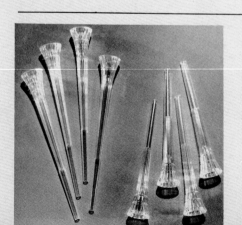

New Crystal-look spiked pillars—pretty and practical
These new pillars were especially designed for the Push-in leg construction of a tier cake, page 14. It's very quick and very easy. Simply take the plate to which the pillars are going to be attached, center it above the iced tier into which the pillars will be attached and gently mark the iced surface by touching the projections on the plate to the icing. Now snap the new spiked pillars to the plate and pierce the tier below as if you were inserting dowel rods. Presto—the tier is secure and the exposed part of the pillars add an attractive sparkle to your tier cake.
303-M-2322. 7" spiked pillars, pack of four
303-M-2324. 9" spiked pillars, pack of four

70

Strong plastic pillars support tiers, fit all Wilton separator plates

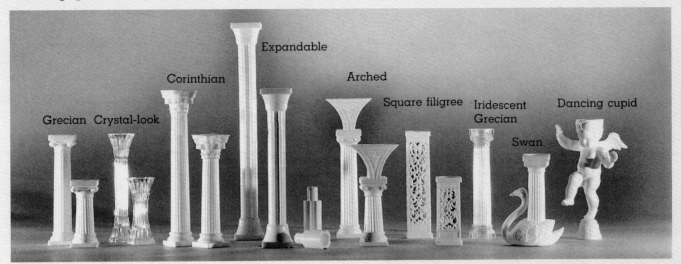

Grecian   Crystal-look   Corinthian   Expandable   Arched   Square filigree   Iridescent Grecian   Swan   Dancing cupid

Grecian pillars. Classic design complements any cake. Add snap-on trims, below, for variety.
303-M-3605. Pack of four 3" pillars
303-M-3702. Pack of four 5" pillars

Crystal-look pillars for sparkling, cut-glass look, airy see-through effect.
303-M-2171. Pack of four 3" pillars
303-M-2196. Pack of four 5" pillars

Corinthian pillars. Graceful columns with ornate capitals. Versatile heights.
303-M-819. Pack of four 5" pillars
303-M-800. Pack of four 7" pillars

Expandable pillars. Have 3", 5", 7", 8" or 10" pillars—just by adding or removing sections! All-purpose!
303-M-1777. Pack of four pillars

Arched pillars for a dramatic old-world look. Harmonize with Arched Pillar tier set, page 69.
303-M-452. Pack of four 4½" pillars
303-M-657. Pack of four 6½" pillars

Square filigree pillars for a lacy, dainty tier cake.
303-M-8070. Pack of four 3" pillars
303-M-7716. Pack of four 5" pillars

Iridescent Grecian pillars—delicate flashes of color on shimmering transparent plastic.
303-M-3257. Pack of four 5" pillars

Swan pillars give an enchanting storybook appearance.
303-M-7724. Pack of four 4" pillars

Dancing cupid pillars add a happy note to your tier cake.
303-M-1210. Pack of four 5½" pillars

Harvest cherub separator set adds a lot of charm to any cake. Chubby little figures rest against 7" pillars. 9" upper plate holds an 8" tier, curved lower plate is 12" across. Set on a 12" square tier or a 14" round tier.
301-M-3517. Complete set

Angelic Serenade separator. A quartet of angel musicians are seated on an antique-look vase. Unique accessory for a shower or wedding cake. Plates are 8" in diameter, total height is 8". Quick way to a beautiful impression.
301-M-607.

Separator plate feet. Glue to any plastic separator plate larger than 6"—you'll have a handy serving tray! Graceful, curved design, strong plastic.
301-M-1247. Set of four feet

Dowel rods. 12" x ¼" diameter, smooth wooden rods. Needed for tier cakes.
399-M-1009. Set of twelve (not shown)

Snap-on trims for pillars.

Cherubs for a romantic accent.
305-M-4104. Pack of 4 for 5" pillars

Filigree adds a delicate lacy frame.
305-M-389. Pack of 4 for 3" pillars
305-M-397. Pack of 4 for 5" pillars

Stud plates glue to separator plates or triple cake circles. Fit all Wilton pillars. White plastic.
301-M-119. Pack of eight

PERFORMANCE PANS®

Reliable classics that come in many sizes, many shapes to give you almost unlimited choices in constructing tier cakes. Durable quality aluminum. Buy pans individually or save on sets.

Round pan set. Most popular shape, in five sizes, 6", 8", 10", 12", 14", each pan is 2" deep.
504-M-118. Save on 5-piece set

Buy individual round pans
2105-M-2185. 6" pan
2105-M-2193. 8" pan
2105-M-2207. 10" pan
2105-M-2215. 12" pan
2105-M-3947. 14" pan
2105-M-3963. 16" pan

Square pan set. For tailored tiers. 8", 10", 12", 14", 16" sizes, each 2" deep.
505-M-104. Save on 5-piece set

Buy individual square pans
507-M-2180. 6" pan
2105-M-8191. 8" pan
2105-M-8205. 10" pan
2105-M-8213. 12" pan
2105-M-8220. 14" pan
2105-M-8231. 16" pan

Petal pan set. Graceful shape in 6", 9", 12" and 15" diameter pans. Each pan is 2" deep.
2105-M-2134. Save on 4-piece set

Buy individual petal pans
2105-M-4346. 6" pan
2105-M-5109. 9" pan
2105-M-5117. 12" pan
2105-M-4344. 15" pan

Hexagon pan set. Bake angled tiers in 6", 9", 12", 15" pans, each 2" deep.
2105-M-3572. Save on 4-piece set

Buy individual hexagon pans
2105-M-5122. 6" pan
2105-M-5125. 9" pan
2105-M-5133. 12" pan
2105-M-5136. 15" pan

Heart Pan set. 6", 9", 12" and 15" pans, each 2" deep for romantic tier cakes.
504-M-207. Save on 4-piece set

Buy individual heart pans.
2105-M-4781. 6" pan
2105-M-5176. 9" pan
2105-M-5168. 12" pan
2105-M-4609. 15" pan

Heart mini-tier set. 5", 7½", 9" pans, 1½" deep plus two plastic plates, six 4½" clear twist legs.
2105-M-409. Heart mini-tier set

Round mini-tier set. 5", 6½", 8" pans, 1½" deep, plus 2 plastic plates, eight 4½" clear twist legs.
2105-M-98042. Round mini-tier set

Round pans

Square pans

Petal pans

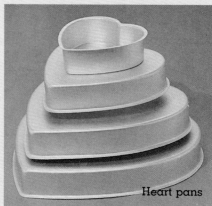

Heart pans

Hexagon pans

Round mini-tier

Heart mini-tier

Ring pans

Ring pans shape unique tier cakes—see page 13. Use, too, for gelatins, party cakes, ice cream. Each pan 3" deep.
2105-M-190. 8" ring pan
2105-M-4013. 10½" ring pan

Bevel pan set. Bakes layers with slanted edges. 8", 10" and 12" top pans—14" and 16" base pans. Five pans in set.
517-M-1200. Bevel pan set

Bevel pans

For information on purchasing products, please see inside front cover

OVENCRAFT™ PANS

Just like professionals use! Sides of all pans are perfectly straight, corners of square and sheet pans are a true 90°. Extra-heavy guage aluminum gives perfect baking results—the smooth anodized finish lets baked tiers slide out easily.

2″ deep round pans
2105-M-5601. 6″ round
2105-M-5602. 8″ round
2105-M-5603. 10″ round
2105-M-5604. 12″ round
2105-M-5605. 14″ round
2105-M-5606. 16″ round

2³/₁₆″ deep square pans.
2105-M-5611. 8″ square
2105-M-5612. 10″ square
2105-M-5613. 12″ square
2105-M-5614. 14″ square

2³/₁₆″ deep sheet pans
2105-M-5615. 7″x11″ sheet
2105-M-5616. 9″x13″ sheet
2105-M-5617. 11″x15″ sheet
2105-M-5618. 12″x18″ sheet

3″ deep round pans
Bakes tiers to two-layer height.
2105-M-5607. 8″ round
2105-M-5608. 10″ round
2105-M-5609. 12″ round
2105-M-5610. 14″ round

2″ deep round

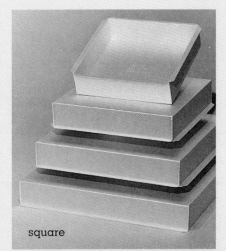
square

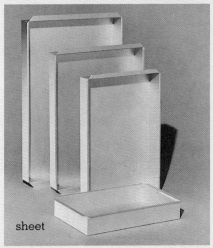
sheet

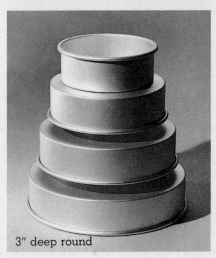
3″ deep round

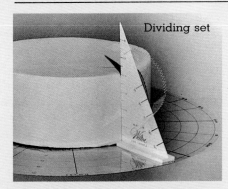
Dividing set

Cake circles

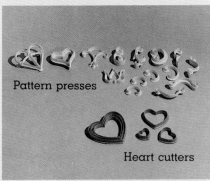
Pattern presses

Heart cutters

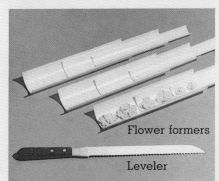
Flower formers

Leveler

Decorator's helpers

Cake dividing set measures any tier quickly, easily.
409-M-800. Triangle marks garlands

Cake circles. Sturdy corrugated cardboard. Indispensable for all cakes.
2104-M-64. 6″ pack of ten
2104-M-80. 8″ pack of twelve
2104-M-102. 10″ pack of twelve
2104-M-129. 12″ pack of eight
2104-M-145. 14″ pack of six
2104-M-160. 16″ pack of six

15-pc. pattern press set imprints designs on tiers. Time-savers!
2104-M-2172. Sturdy plastic

Heart cutter set. Handy as pattern presses to imprint designs.
2304-M-115. Plastic. 6 sizes

Flower formers. Flowers dry in natural curves, look prettier.
417-M-9500. 11″ long, set of nine

Serrated leveler. 12″ steel blade levels tiers. Handy kitchen helper.
409-M-1016. Rosewood handle

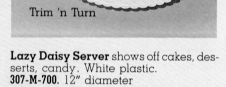

Lazy Daisy

Professional

Trim 'n Turn

Filigree Bridge and Stairway set
Adds drama and excitement to tier cakes, makes them much more impressive. Use with a single cake or join satellite cakes to main cake. Tops of tapered stairs push easily into tiers or snap into bridge. Use bridge to hold ornament or flowers, set figures on stairs. Page 51 shows how to use. Stairs 16¾" long, bridge area 4¾" x 5". Lacy white plastic. Set of 2 stairways, one bridge.
205-M-2109. Save on set
205-M-1218. Stairway only
205-M-1234. Bridge only

Lazy Daisy Server shows off cakes, desserts, candy. White plastic.
307-M-700. 12" diameter

Professional Turntable. Heavy-duty aluminum, 12" surface, turns easily.
307-M-2501. Lifetime tool

Trim 'n Turn Cake Stand. Easy ball-bearing action, holds up to 100 pounds. 12" diameter, plastic.
2103-M-2518. Easy to store

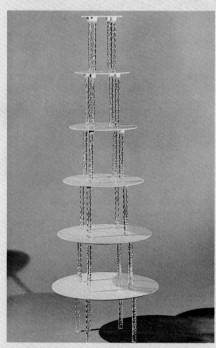

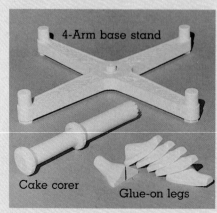

4-Arm base stand

Cake corer

Glue-on legs

Crystal Clear Divider set gives strong support to lofty cakes with no dowels needed. Includes six white plastic plates, 6", 8", 10", 12", 14" and 16". Also 24 clear plastic legs, 7½" high.
301-M-9450. Save on set
302-M-9730. 6" plate
302-M-9749. 8" plate
302-M-9757. 10" plate
302-M-9765. 12" plate
302-M-9773. 14" plate
302-M-9780. 16" plate

303-M-9794. Pack of four 7½" legs
303-M-977. Pack of four 9" legs

Tall Tier Stand set supports up to six tiers—no need for dowels! Quick way to beautiful cakes—see pages 6 through 12. Set includes five 6½" columns with one bottom and one top bolt, 18" footed base plate, 16", 14", 12", 10" and 8" plates. Strong white plastic, lacy openwork edges.
304-M-7915. Save on set!

302-M-7894. 8" plate
302-M-7908. 10" plate
302-M-7924. 12" plate
302-M-7940. 14" plate
302-M-7967. 16" plate
302-M-7983. 18" plate

303-M-7910. 6½" column
304-M-5009. 7¾" column
303-M-703. 13½" column

304-M-7923. Top column cap nut
304-M-7930. Glue-on plate legs
304-M-7941. Bottom column bolt

4-Arm Base Stand lets you add four satellite cakes on 8", 10" or 12" plates. Sturdy plastic. Includes base bolt.
304-M-8245. 4-Arm base
304-M-8253. Base bolt only

Cake Corer removes tier center quickly. Page 6 shows how to use. Plastic.
304-M-8172. Handy tool

Wilton®
Wedding Cake Porcelains

Heirloom-quality porcelain figures . . . treasured keepsakes.

Promise. Clear crystal-look heart set off by delicate ribboned blooms forms a romantic back drop for this porcelain couple. 7¼" high.
117-M-311. Pink
117-M-309. Blue
117-M-307. Lilac

Captivation. A silken canopy shelters this porcelain bridal couple. A carpet of baby roses completes the romantic setting. 10" high.
117-M-254. White
117-M-211. Lilac
117-M-238. Pink

Devotion. Porcelain bridal couple pause for one serene moment before a fairy castle window of transparent arched panes. 8½" high.
117-M-425. White
117-M-421. Pink
117-M-423. Lilac

Rhapsody. Crystal-look bells chime softly above porcelain bridal couple. Flowers, ribbons and crystal look base add elegant touches. 9½" high.
117-M-305. Pink
117-M-303. Lilac
117-M-301. White

Cherish. Porcelain with deep porcelain base to which accompanying brass plate can be engraved and attached. Plate slips in base slot. 8½" high.
117-M-190. Yellow
117-M-157. Pink
117-M-173. Lilac

Reflection. Three transparent panels accented by only a deft touch of ribbon and cover of flowers. Porcelain couple. Ornament is 8¼" high.
117-M-297. Pink
117-M-130. Blue
117-M-270. Lilac

For information on purchasing products, please see inside front cover

Chapel bells. Elegant in its simplicity. Satin bells set off by a puff of white tulle and clusters of flowers. 9" high.
103-M-2419. Ivory
103-M-2413. White
103-M-2415. Pink
103-M-2411. Lilac
103-M-2417. Blue

Rosebud brilliance. The bride and groom are set off to perfection in this fairyland openwork gazebo. Lovebirds serenade the happy couple from the domed roof top and flowers bloom in the path of the joyful pair. 8½" high.
101-M-44315. Black coat
101-M-44323. White Coat

Hearts take wing. This is an ornament often kept and admired years after the blissful wedding day. The symbolic heart with its lacy, filigree border and filmy tulle trim forms a delightful background for the graceful white lovebirds. 10½" high.
103-M-6218

Moonbeam's embrace. Handsome bridal couple in keepsake bisque porcelain pause under double archways of glowing white flowers and silvery leaves. Flowers in profusion cascade down to white filigree plastic base. 10½" high.
112-M-1000. White coat
112-M-2000. Black coat

Sweet ceremony. The flaring mouth of a large, glitter-covered chapel bell shelters the beautiful bridal couple. A large beaded heart, accented by a pouf of tulle completes the charming setting. 10" high.
101-M-22011. Black coat
101-M-22028. White coat

Spellbound. Starry-eyed bridal couple embrace in a romantic, old world gazebo, as white lovebirds look down from above. Flower-covered vines provide a colorful frame for the entranced pair. Ornament is 9" high.
110-M-406. Yellow flowers
110-M-422. Pink flowers

Heart-to-heart. Slight departure from the usual couple but very cute! Couple is encircled by two large white plastic hearts—heart in background is in intricate open work with a heart "window" in its center. Both hearts are trimmed with delicate white lace. 9½" high.
110-M-376.

Rose cascade. This charming couple, fashioned in keepsake-quality bisque porcelain, is resplendent under a bower of spring flowers that cascade from a cloud of tulle. A beautiful memento of the joyous wedding day! 10" high.
112-M-8000. Black coat
112-M-9000. White coat

Harmony. Handsome black couple stands tall before an openwork white plastic heart—made more dramatic by a border of ruffled white tulle. Bells and miniature white roses complete the elegant trim. 9½" high.
116-M-100. Black coat
116-M-200. White coat

Mantilla. Quiet elegance. Against the flower bedecked backdrop of a tall cathedral window adorned with a golden cross the handsome bridal couple share a blissful moment on this happy day. An impressive 11" high.
114-M-45416. Black coat
114-M-45424. White coat

Morning rosebud. Fluttering doves of peace greet the nuptial pair as they pass through classic grillwork gates. Fabric flowers bloom on the couple's path and around the embossed plastic heart base. 8" high.
101-M-44013. Black coat
101-M-44020. White coat

Circles of love. The circle, considered from ancient times to be the sign of eternity, symbolizes everlasting love. Two side-by-side rings, framed by a beautiful arch of flowers put this message in a modern setting. A simple, but beautiful keepsake. 10" high.
103-M-9004

Tender heart. Bisque porcelain figures. Cherished mementos. 9″ high.
112-M-200. Black coat—pink flowers
112-M-300. Black coat—blue flowers
112-M-100. Black coat—white flowers
112-M-500. White coat—pink flowers
112-M-400. White coat—blue flowers
112-M-600. White coat—white flowers

Spring song. Two snowy-white birds in a true fairyland setting perch under a bower of luxuriant flowers. Under the boughs a cloud of fluffy white tulle floats above the filigree heart base. Birds are beautifully sculptured—perfect for a spring wedding. 9½″ high.
111-M-2802

Circles of lace. Enraptured couple enjoy a magic interlude in a dream setting. Six laced-covered arcs curve gently to a dome where a cloud of tulle envelopes a rose and bell. For the bride who likes a dainty old-fashioned look. 12″ high.
114-M-8014. Black coat
114-M-8022. White coat

ANNIVERSARY ORNAMENTS
highlight happy years of married life

Petite anniversary

Anniversary years

Double ring devotion

Anniversary waltz

50 years of happiness

Petite anniversary. Sculptured silver and gold wreaths for 25th and 50th celebrations. 6¾″ high.
105-M-4265. Silver anniversary
105-M-4273. Golden anniversary

Anniversary years. Filigree wreath holds easy snap-out numbers that match wreath—5, 10, 15 and 40. 5¾″ high. Trim with flowers or ribbons.
105-M-4257

Double ring devotion. Rings and dress coordinated to match 25th and 50th silver and gold colors. 5¼″
105-M-4613. Silver anniversary
105-M-4605. Golden anniversary

Anniversary waltz. Color of wreath, top bow and dress coordinated. 9″ high.
102-M-5527. Golden anniversary
102-M-5519. Silver anniversary

50 years of happiness a glorious ornament suited to the importance of the occasion. A shining wreath displays the impressive anniversary number being celebrated. Wreath on its classic white filigree heart base is encircled by blossoms and silver or gold leaves. 10″high.
102-M-223. Golden anniversary
102-M-207. Silver anniversary

78

DAINTY PETITE ORNAMENTS to crown a cake
or place within pillars. Charming keepsakes.

Petite Happy hearts. Classic keepsake in bisque porcelain. 6½" high.
108-M-219. White coat-pink ribbon
108-M-211. White coat-blue ribbon
108-M-215. White coat-lilac ribbon
108-M-213. Black coat-lilac ribbon
108-M-209. Black coat-blue ribbon
108-M-217. Black coat-pink ribbon

Petite Tender heart. Charming bisque porcelain couple backed by laced-edged heart with filigree border. A lasting memento. 5½" high.
108-M-522. Blond-white coat
108-M-524. Blond-black coat
108-M-422. Black couple—white coat
108-M-324. Black couple—black coat

Petite Elegance. Lustrous satin bells hang from a filigree heart. Pearlized stamens set off flowers. 5¼" high.
106-M-343. Pink ribbon
106-M-349. Lilac ribbon
106-M-347. Blue ribbon
106-M-341. Ivory ribbon
106-M-345. White ribbon

Petite Double ring. Straightforward expression of classic simplicity with doves of peace fluttering above twin nuptial rings. Gossamer wisps of cloudlike tulle gently float above the filigree heart base—all symbols of perfect wedded bliss. 6½" high.
106-M-4316

Petite Spring song. Happily chirping love birds, perched beneath a bower of radiant spring flowers, prepare to sing love's sweetest song. A romantic arch of perfect blossoms rises above the white filigree base of joined hearts. Ideal for a spring wedding cake. 7" high.
106-M-159

La belle petite. A single, perfect flower shines through a mist of white tulle. Framed by an open heart, a dainty filigree bell magically sends out both heavenly chimes and a cascade of satiny flowers. Classically beautiful crown for a small bridal cake. 5½" high.
106-M-248

Adoration

Natural beauty

PETITE ORNAMENTS

Unique collection of show-piece ornaments, perfectly proportioned for smaller cakes. Or set one within tall pillars for a charming little tableau.

Natural beauty. Two love-birds, perched in front of a flower bedecked and be-ribboned filigree heart, sing love's sweet song. White filigree base.

106-M-1163. White
106-M-1120. Pink
106-M-1147. Lilac
106-M-1104. Peach

Double ring couple

Bells of joy

Petite Adoration. Three gift-bearing cherubs celebrate the happy day in a joyful dance. Ornament is just 4½" high, ideal for use as a fanciful focal point when placed between tiers. Also perfect to top the small tier being saved for the couple's first anniversary. Beautifully embossed base in pure white plastic.
111-M-141

Petite Double ring couple. Lovebirds flutter above the symbolic wedding bands and serve as the background for the happy couple. The pretty scene is set on a dainty white plastic base.
104-M-42413. Black coat
104-M-42420. White coat

Petite Bells of joy. Dainty lace-trimmed bands encircle four rose-topped filigree bells, as a cloud of soft white tulle floats above. 6½" high.
106-M-2658

Lovers in lace

Dainty charm

Petite Lovers in lace. Ruffled lace-covered rings topped by a puff of filmy white tulle form a romantic bower for this handsome couple. A beautiful and tradi-tional ornament to grace any cake. Heart scroll base. 7" high.
104-M-818. Black coat
104-M-826. White coat

Petite Dainty charm. Neatly arranged floral spray seems to float in a cloud of tulle that sets off the handsome couple. Sure to be a cherished memento of the bride. 5½" high. Black coat only.
104-M-32310. White
104-M-1172. Lilac
104-M-1156. Pink

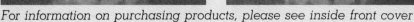

For information on purchasing products, please see inside front cover

CAKE COTTAGE SCHOOL OF CAKE DECORATING

BALTIMORE, MARYLAND

Certificate of Award

This is to certify that:

Gerry Stotler

has completed the

Basic Course _____ in Cake Decorating.

In witness thereof this certificate is awarded this 19 day of December 19 85.

the Cake Cottage

_____
Instructor

_____
Director

LITHO IN U.S.A.

© GOES 745